'Deadweight (tonnage) is a unit used to measure how much weight a ship can carry. It is the sum of the weights of cargo, fuel, fresh water, ballast water, provisions, passengers and crew. Instead of using it to ensure the ship stays afloat and moves seamlessly, I want to use it to figure out its tipping point, which is the possibility to sink it, destroy it and free its cargo in the process.' DOMINIQUE WHITE

"Il tonnellaggio di portata lorda è un'unità di misura utilizzata per calcolare il peso che una nave può trasportare. È la somma dei pesi di merci, carburante, acqua dolce, acqua di zavorra, provviste, passeggeri e equipaggio. Invece di usarla per garantire che la nave rimanga a galla e navighi senza problemi, voglio usarla per capire il suo punto di ribaltamento, ovvero la possibilità di affondarla, distruggerla e liberarne il carico". DOMINIQUE WHITE

Dominique White is the ninth winner of the Max Mara Art Prize for Women 2022–24. Founded in 2005, the Prize provides an artist with the generous opportunities of time, space and funding, awarding them with a six-month residency in Italy. The residency, organised by the Collezione Maramotti, was tailored to White's interests and followed by the commission of a new work of art inspired by the experience. *Deadweight*, the culmination of this Prize, is launched at Whitechapel Gallery in London and will tour to Collezione Maramotti, Reggio Emilia, Italy.

Sculptor and installation artist Dominique White draws inspiration from the symbolism and transformative power of the sea. Her artworks explore the tension between ghostly fragility and heavy physical presence, often incorporating discarded maritime artefacts like sails, masts, weathered wood and rope, as well as materials such as clay and untreated iron. White's winning proposal for the Max Mara Art Prize reimagined the maritime concept of 'deadweight tonnage', traditionally associated with a ship's stability, to explore the possibilities of disruption and liberation.

Over the six months of her residency, White travelled across Italy, engaging with experts and exploring maritime histories to inform her artistic vision. In Agnone, in the Molise region of Italy, White deepened her understanding of the process involved in casting and pouring bronze. She undertook a week-long workshop at the historic Pontificia Fonderia di Campane Marinelli, a family-run bell foundry founded more than a thousand years ago. In the ancient Sicilian capital of Palermo, White met with Giovanna Fiume, a renowned historian and former professor of modern history, to explore the intersection of ship navigation technology with colonialism. In Genoa, under the tutelage of professors Claudia Tacchella and Massimo Corradi, who specialise in construction science and history, she visited significant naval and archaeological museums and archives and undertook a concentrated investigation into how ships are built, as well as shipbuilding terminology, which is intimately connected to the human cycle: birth, life and death. In Milan she participated in a workshop at Fonderia Artistica Battaglia, honing her skills in the centuries-old tradition of creating handmade bronze artefacts using an intricate lost-wax casting technique.

During the concluding phase of her residency, White was based in Todi, Umbria, refining her metalworking skills under the mentorship of Michele Ciribifera, former assistant to sculptor Beverly Pepper. Engaged in intensive studio work, White delved into novel techniques and approaches, actively experimenting with metal fabrication processes.

Showcasing four sculptural pieces, *Deadweight* marries strength with delicacy. The angular forms are forged from rusted iron, organic remnants of sisal, raffia, driftwood and kaolin clay. They conjure images of anchors, a ship's hull and skeletal marine remains. A notable innovation of the installation is White's immersion of the sculptures in the Mediterranean Sea. This poetic gesture examines the sea's continual transformative impact on materials.

White's artistic methodology integrates theories of Black subjectivity, Afropessimism and hydrarchy from below, disrupting the conventional dynamics of power gained over land through water. White reconceptualises the notion of 'shipwreck(ed)' as both a reflexive act and a state of existence, interrogating established power structures and evoking narratives of rebellion and liberation.

White has described the core of her practice as the capacity and the courage to 'dream of new worlds in the unknown […] It's a reminder that there isn't only one future, or one interpretation of how the world should be.'

Dominique White è la nona vincitrice del Max Mara Art Prize for Women 2022–24. Fondato nel 2005, il premio offre a un'artista generose opportunità di tempo, spazio e finanziamenti, premiandola con una residenza di sei mesi in Italia. La residenza, organizzata dalla Collezione Maramotti, è stata ideata su misura sugli interessi di White e accompagnata dalla commissione di una nuova opera d'arte ispirata all'esperienza. *Deadweight*, il punto di arrivo di questo premio, è presentato prima alla Whitechapel Gallery di Londra e successivamente alla Collezione Maramotti di Reggio Emilia.

Artista che lavora con la scultura e l'installazione, Dominique White trae ispirazione dal simbolismo e dal potere trasformativo del mare. Le sue opere d'arte esplorano la tensione tra una fragilità spettrale e una pesante presenza fisica, spesso incorporando manufatti marittimi dismessi come vele, alberi, legno e cime danneggiati dalle intemperie, oltre a materiali come argilla e ferro non trattato. La proposta vincente di White per il Max Mara Art Prize ha rielaborato il concetto marittimo "deadweight [portata lorda]", tradizionalmente associato alla stabilità di una nave, per esplorare le possibilità di rottura e liberazione.

Nei sei mesi di residenza White ha viaggiato in Italia confrontandosi con esperti ed approfondendo storie marittime per ispirare la sua visione artistica. Ad Agnone, nella regione del Molise, White ha approfondito la conoscenza del processo di fusione e colata del bronzo. Ha inoltre intrapreso un laboratorio di una settimana presso la storica Pontificia Fonderia di Campane Marinelli, una fonderia a conduzione familiare fondata più di mille anni fa. Nell'antica città siciliana di Palermo, White ha conosciuto Giovanna Fiume, già professoressa di Storia Moderna per esplorare i punti di contatto tra la tecnologia di navigazione e il colonialismo. A Genova, sotto la guida dei professori Claudia Tacchella e Massimo Corradi specializzati nella scienza delle costruzioni e nella sua storia, White ha visitato alcuni dei più importanti musei e archivi navali e archeologici, intraprendendo un'indagine incentrata sulla modalità di costruzione delle navi e sulla terminologia navale che è intimamente connessa al ciclo umano: nascita, vita e morte. A Milano ha partecipato a un laboratorio presso la Fonderia Artistica Battaglia, affinando le sue capacità nella tradizione secolare di creare artigianalmente manufatti in bronzo, attraverso la complessa tecnica della fusione a cera persa.

White ha trascorso la fase conclusiva della sua residenza in Italia a Todi, in Umbria, per affinare le sue capacità di lavorazione dei metalli sotto la guida di Michele Ciribifera, ex assistente della scultrice Beverly Pepper. Impegnata in un intenso lavoro in studio, White ha approfondito tecniche e metodi nuovi, sperimentando attivamente i processi di fabbricazione del metallo.

Presentando quattro opere scultoree, *Deadweight* coniuga forza e delicatezza. Le forme angolari sono forgiate con ferro arrugginito, resti organici di sisal, rafia, legname e argilla caolino. Evocano immagini di ancore, lo scafo di una nave e i resti marini scheletrici. Un'importante innovazione dell'opera è rappresentata dall'immersione delle sculture nel Mar Mediterraneo da parte di White. Questo gesto poetico evidenzia il permanente effetto trasformativo del mare sui materiali.

La metodologia artistica di White integra le teorie della soggettività nera, l'afropessimismo e l'idrarchia dal basso, scardinando le convenzionali dinamiche di acquisizione di potere attraverso la terraferma e il mare. White riconcettualizza la nozione di "naufrag(i)o" sia come atto riflessivo che come stato di esistenza, interrogando le strutture di potere consolidate ed evocando narrazioni di ribellione e liberazione.

White ha descritto l'essenza della sua pratica come la capacità e il coraggio di "sognare nuovi mondi nell'ignoto [...] Un promemoria di come non esista un solo futuro, o una sola interpretazione di come dovrebbe essere il mondo".

GILANE TAWADROS, DIRECTOR, WHITECHAPEL GALLERY
KATRINA SCHWARZ, CURATOR: SPECIAL PROJECTS, WHITECHAPEL GALLERY

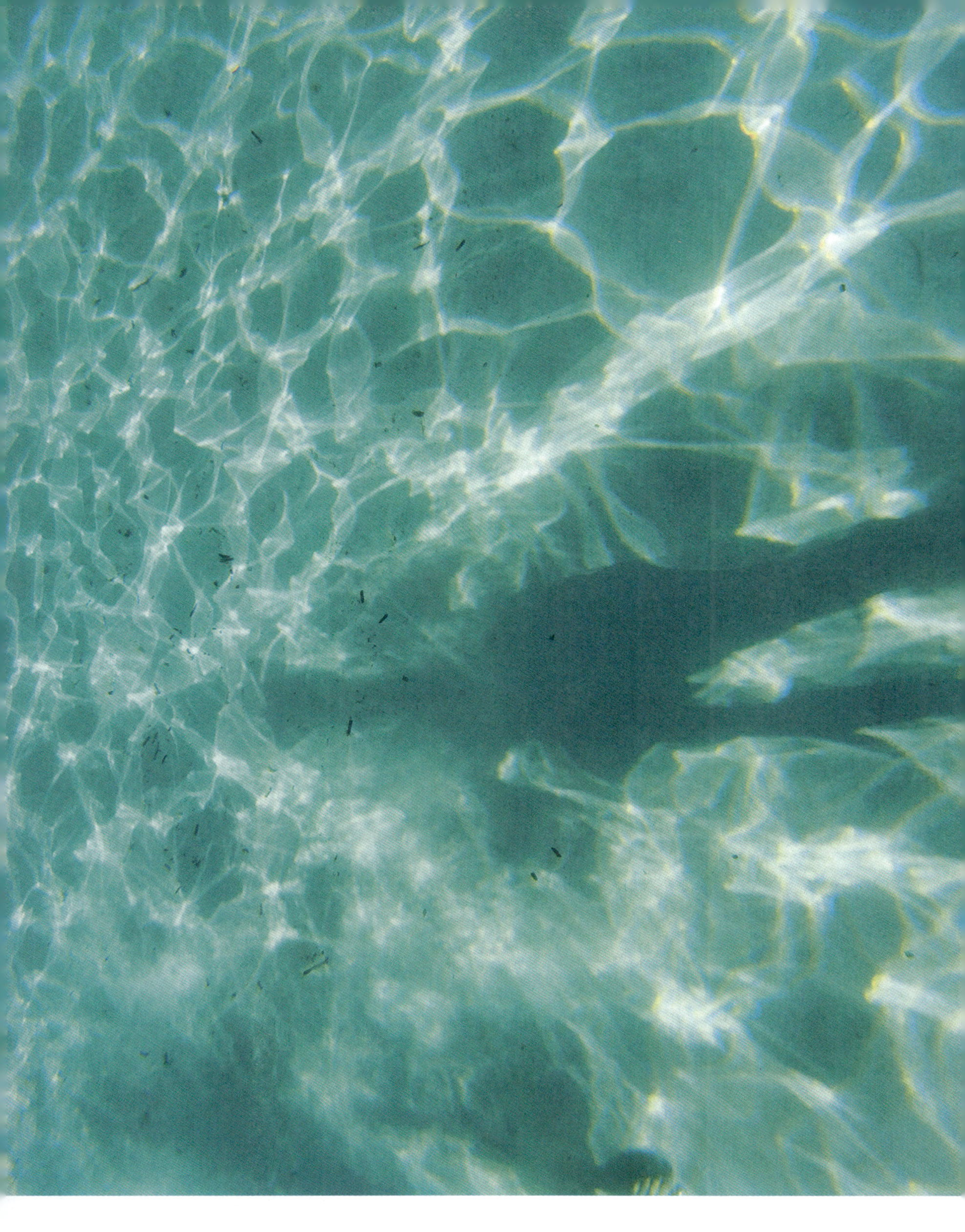

Self-portrait / Autoritratto. Dominique White. (Sicily, July / Sicilia, luglio 2019)

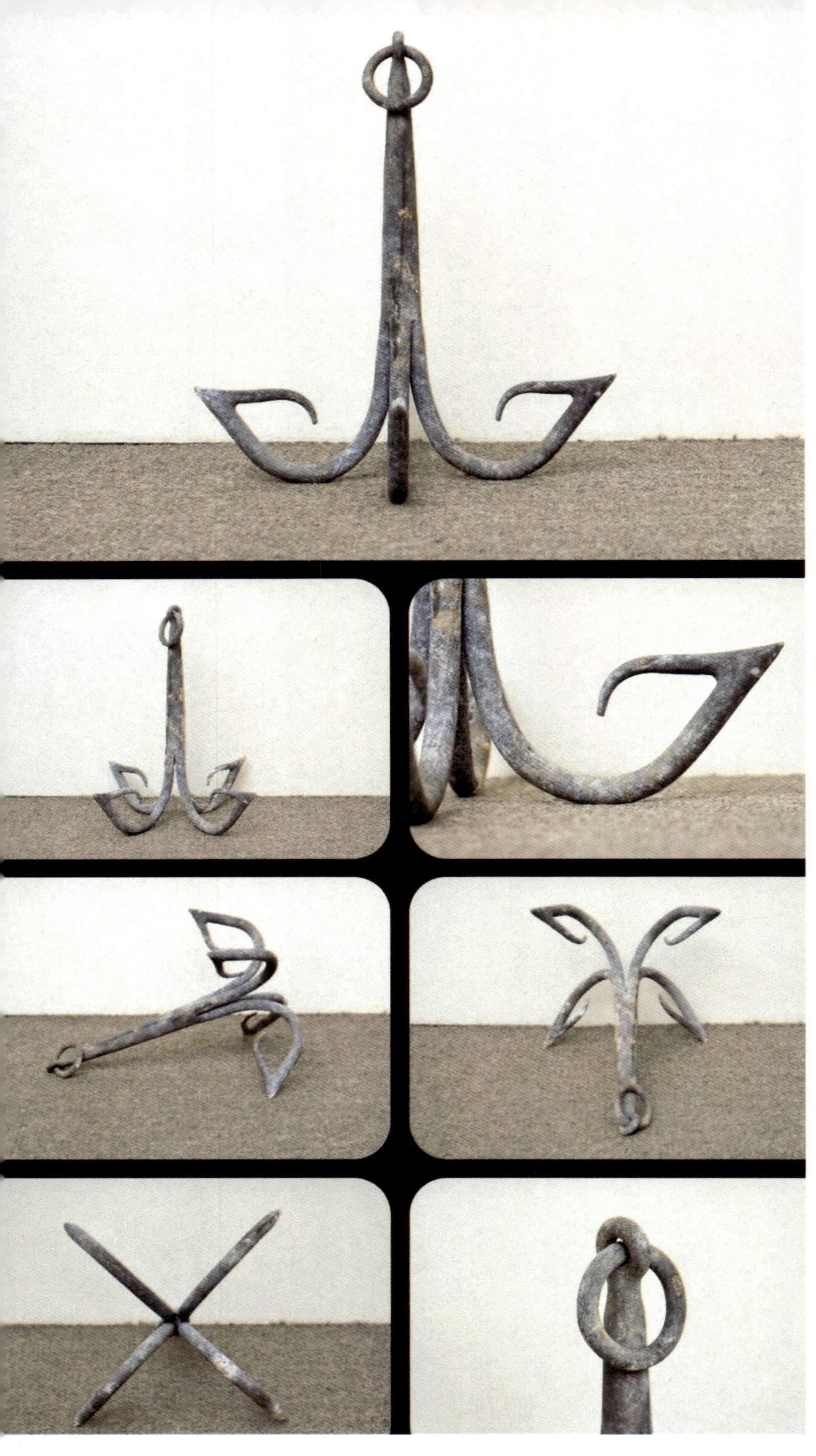

Screenshot of anchor from an auction / Screenshot di un'ancora all'asta

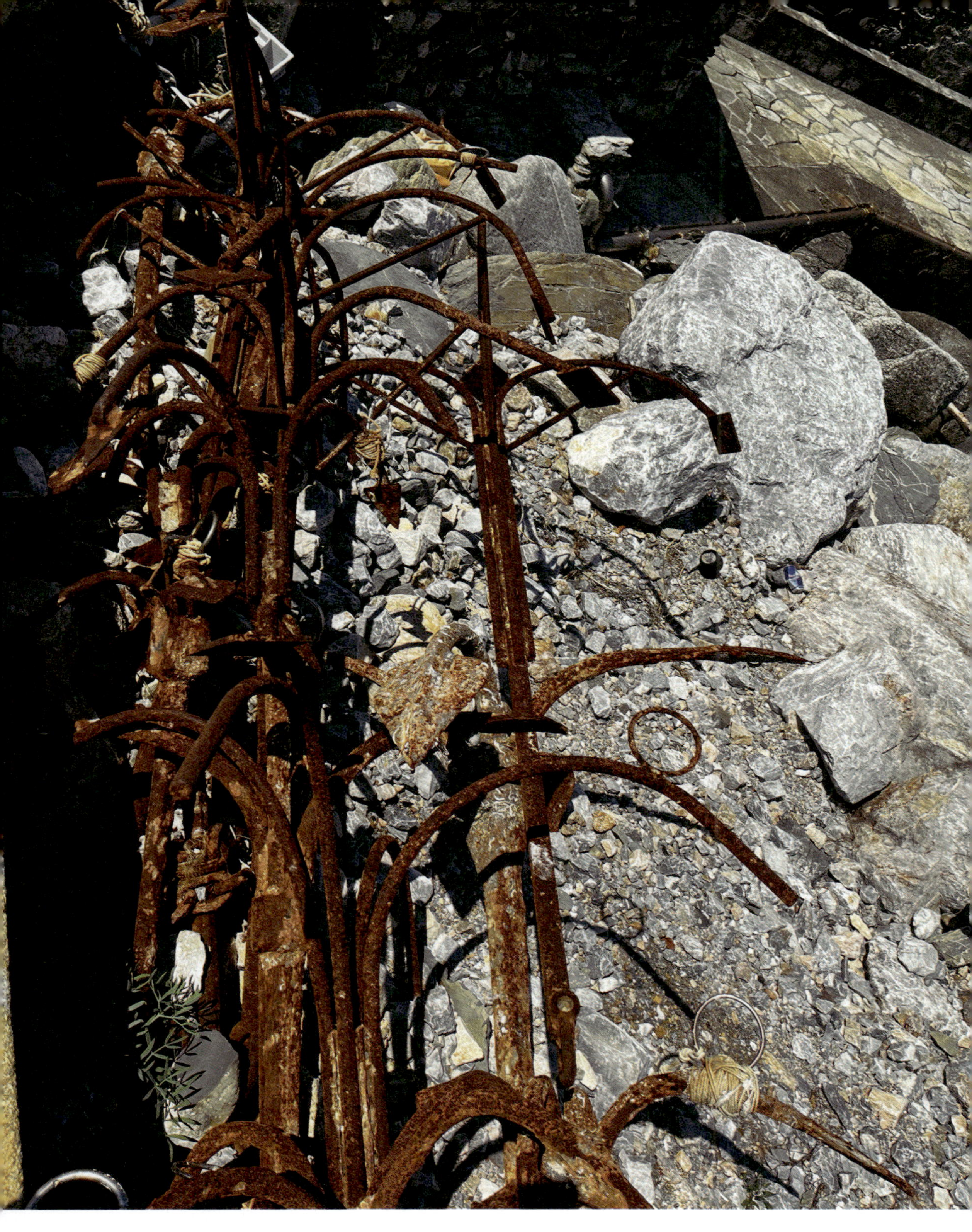

Abandoned anchors in Genoa (Italy, July 2023) / Ancore abbandonate a Genova (Italia, luglio 2023)

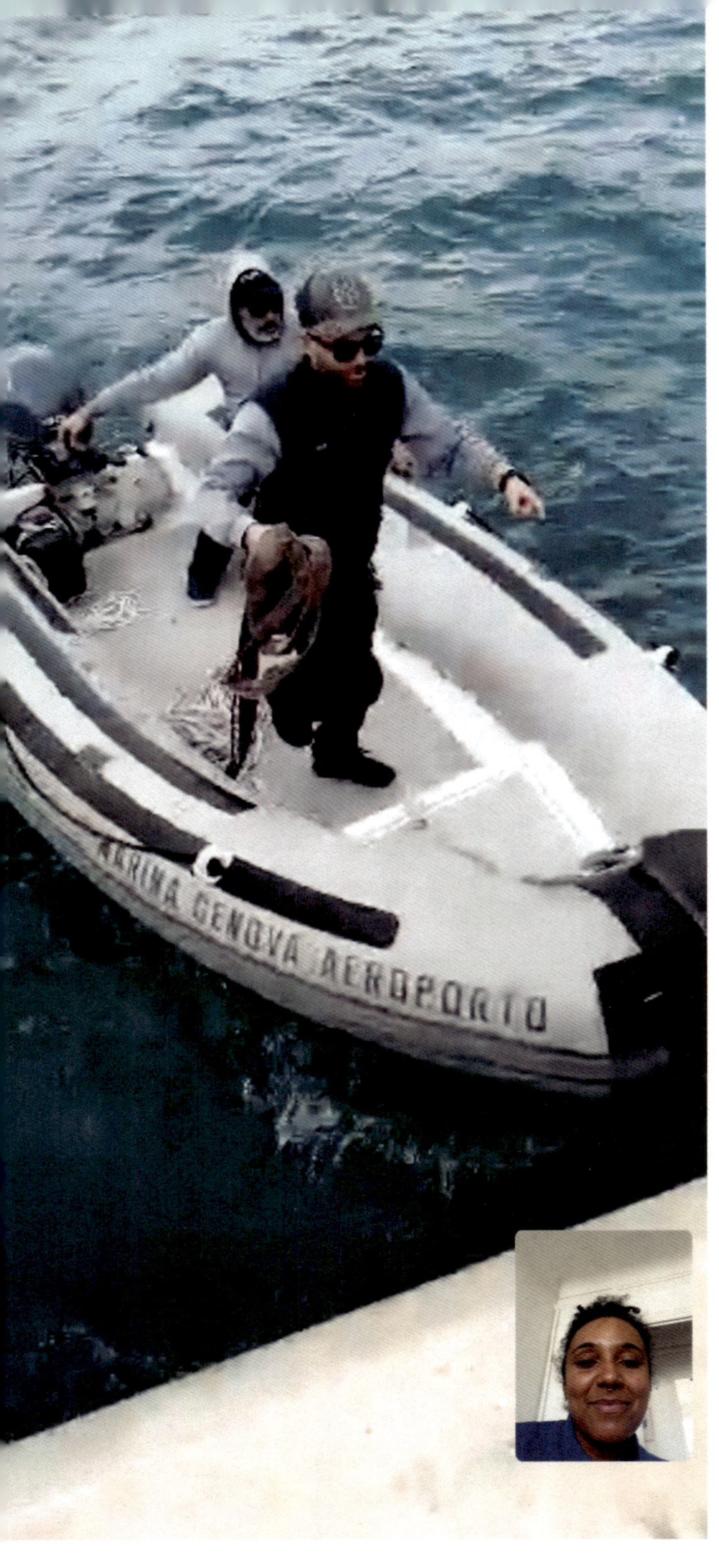

FaceTime between the Mediterranean Sea (Italy) and Clermont-Ferrand (France) (February 2024)
Facetime tra il Mar Mediterraneo (Italia) e Clermont-Ferrand (Francia) (febbraio 2024)

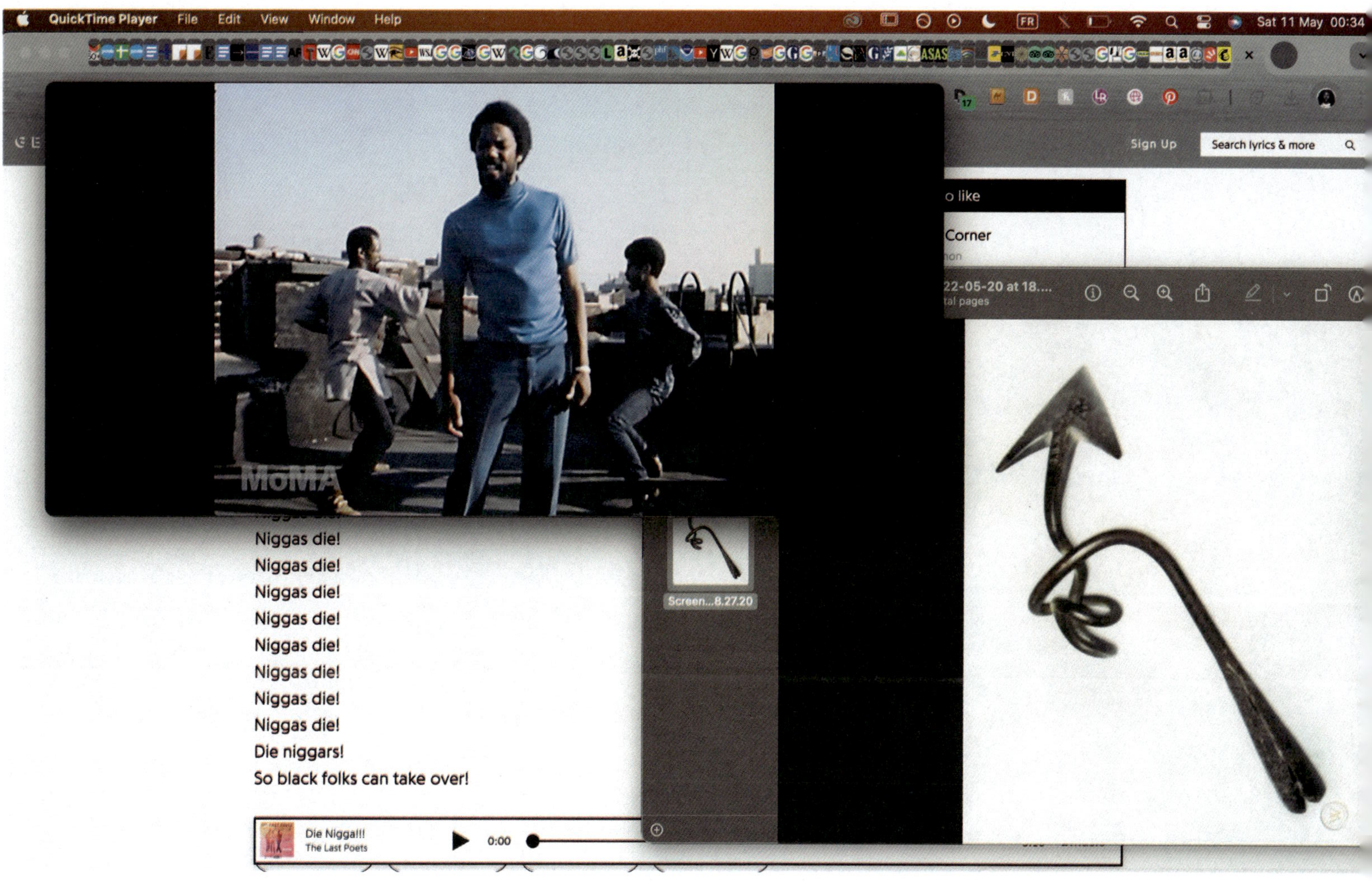

Screenshot from White's computer (May 2024) / Screenshot dal computer di White (maggio 2024)

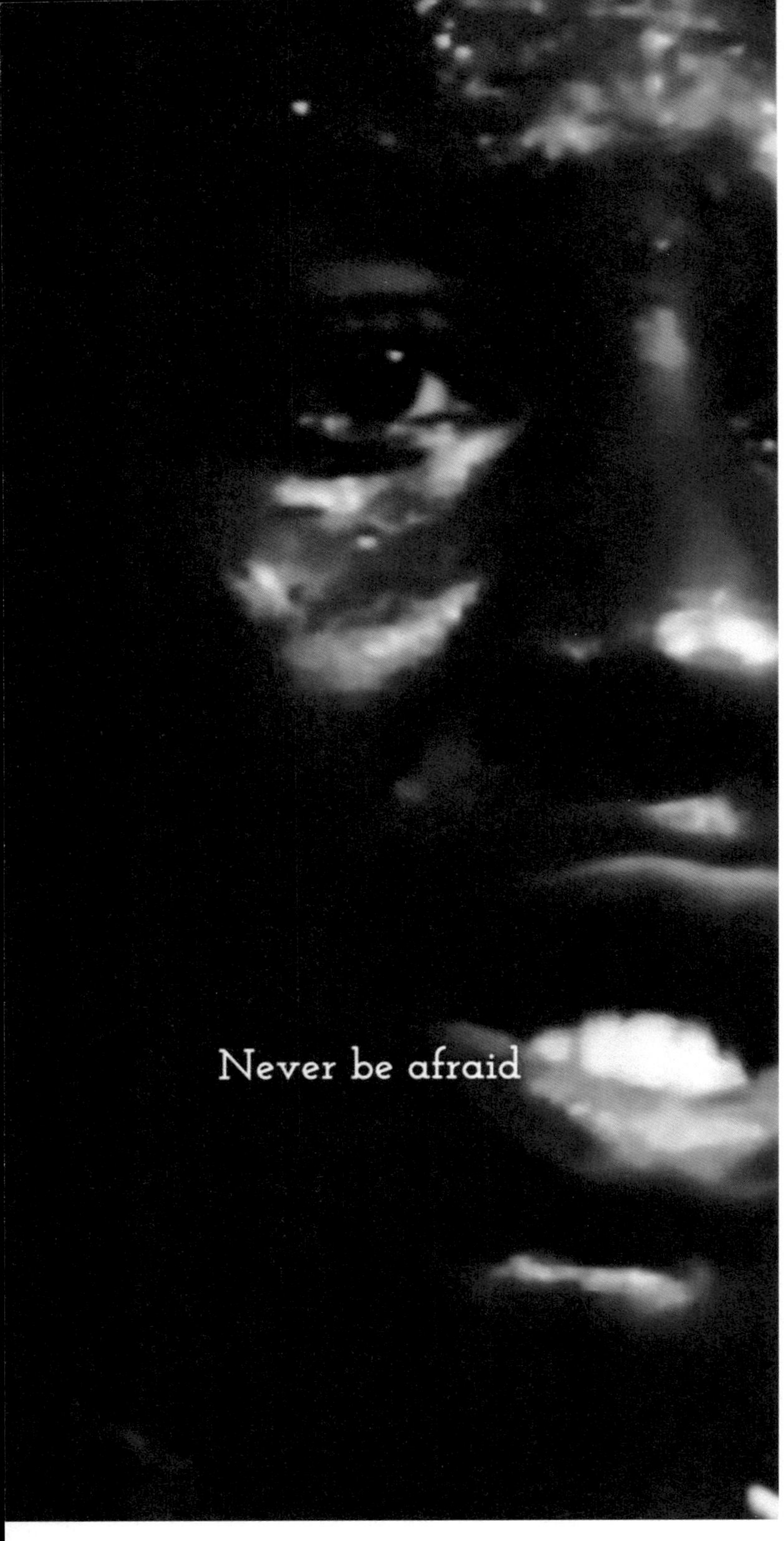

Screenshot from White's iPhone (May 2024) / Screenshot dall'iPhone di White (maggio 2024)

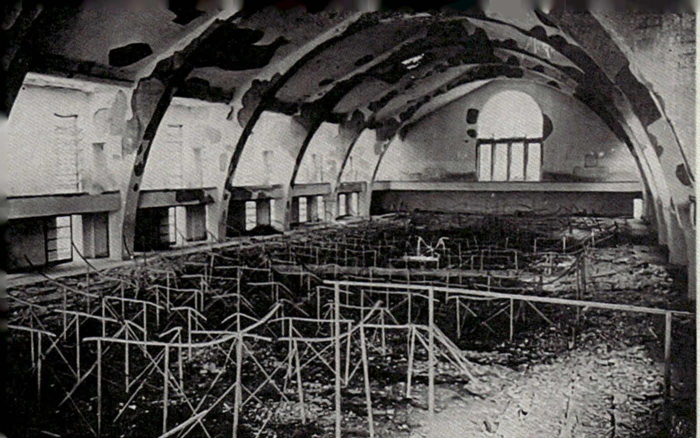

Distruzione delle navi e danneggiamento delle strutture a causa dell'incendio.
Ships destruction and structures damages caused by fire.

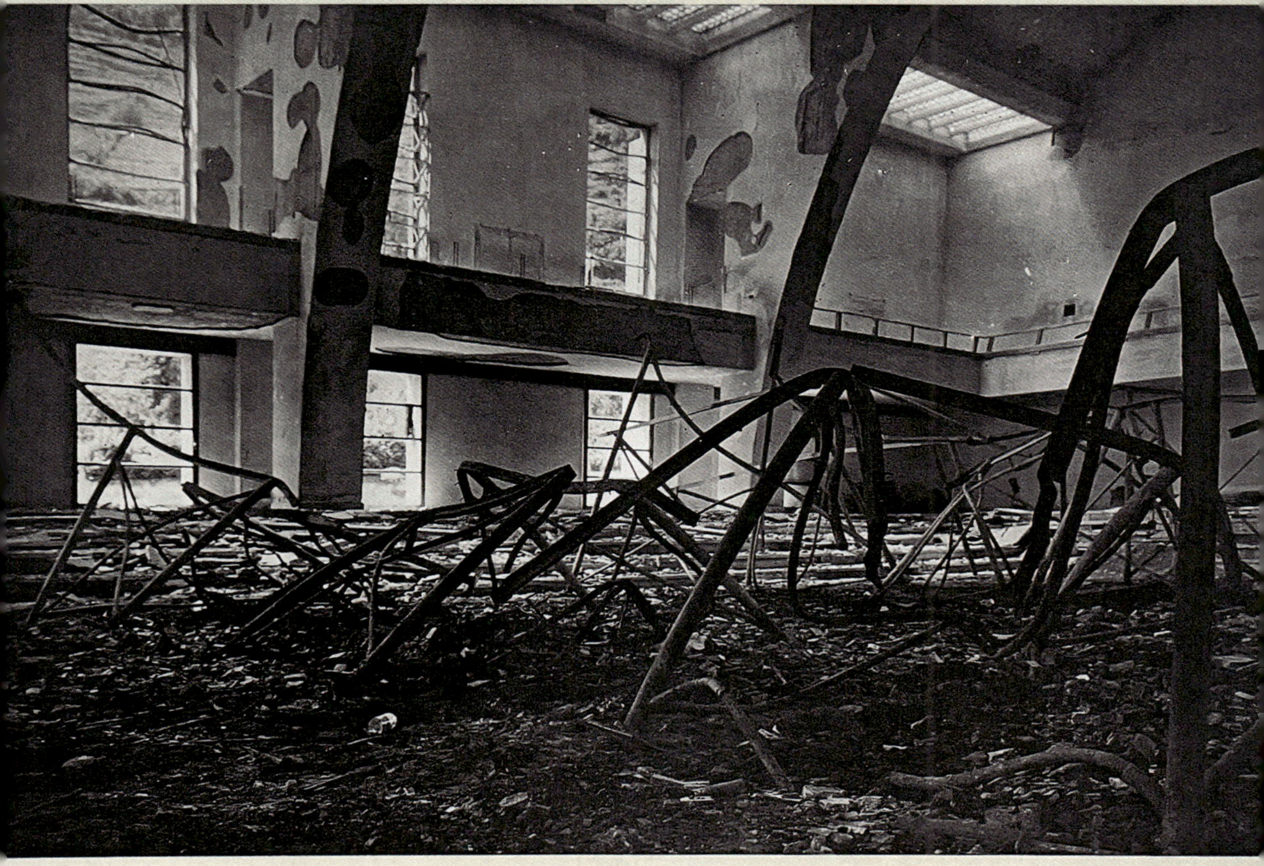

LA DOCUMENTAZIONE

Tutte le operazioni di recupero venivano documentate graficamente e fotograficamente con notevole precisione e meticolosità.

In particolare l'Ing. G. Ucelli, che seguì scrupolosamente i lavori, annotò e raccolse una mole enorme di documenti, dalle notizie circa i più antichi tentativi di recupero, alla propaganda giornalistica prima, durante e dopo i lavori, alle indagini geologiche, idrogeologiche, chimiche, paleobotaniche, ecc..
Parte della documentazione da lui personalmente raccolta in un archivio, che successivamente la famiglia ha

THE DOCUMENTS

All the recovering operations were graphically and photographically documented with remarkable precision and meticulousness. Particularly the engineer G. Ucelli, who followed scrupulously the work, noted and collected an enormous quantity of documents, from the news about the most ancient recovery attempts, to the journalist propaganda previous, contemporary and succeeding the works, to the geological, hydro-geological, chemical, palaeobotanical inquiries etc... A part of the documentation was collected by him in an archive, which was afterwards generously donated from the family to the state and, mcored in the text "Nemi's ships

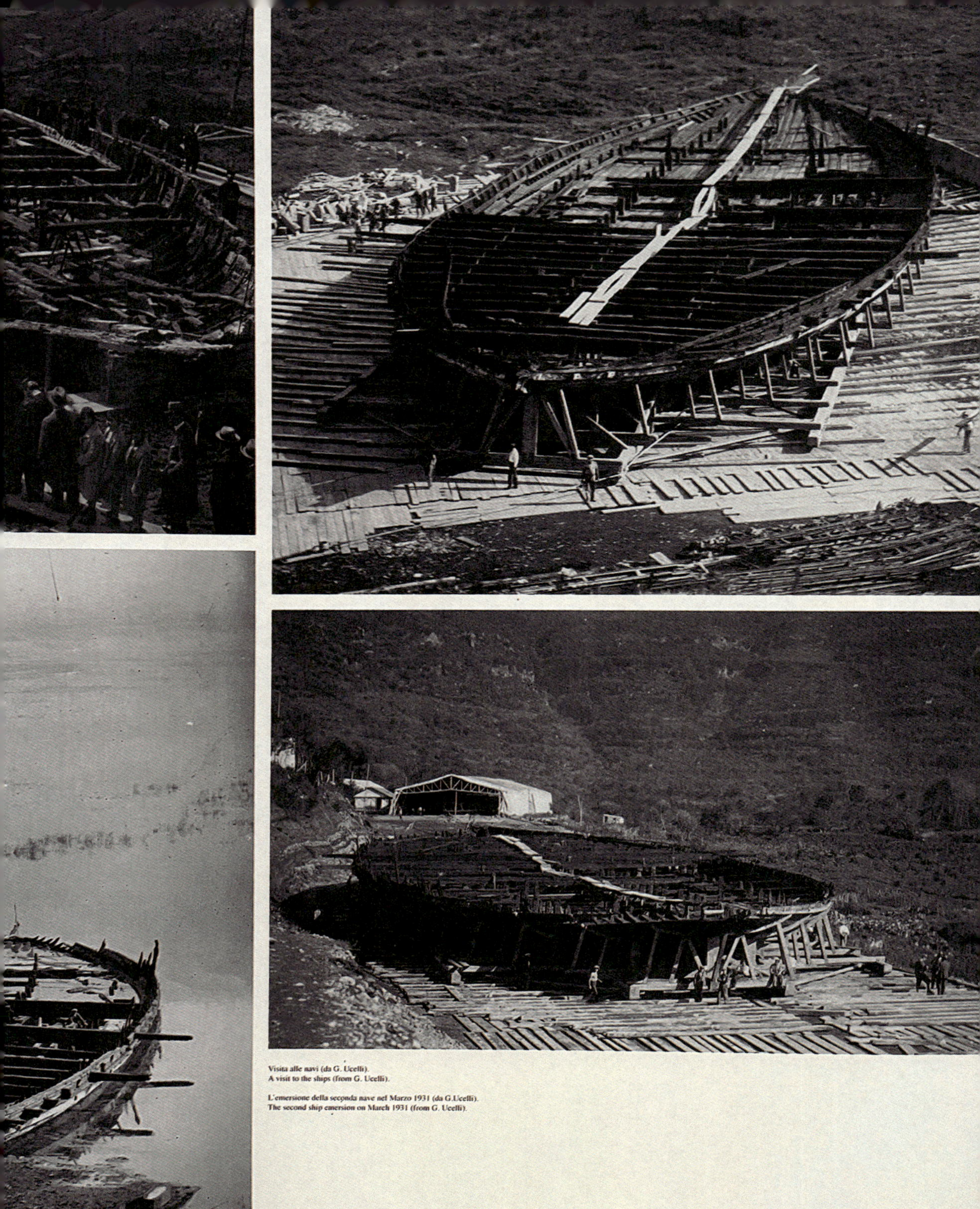

Partial replica of an information panel in / Riproduzione parziale di un pannello informativo nel Museo delle Navi Romane (Italy, August / Italia, agosto 2023)

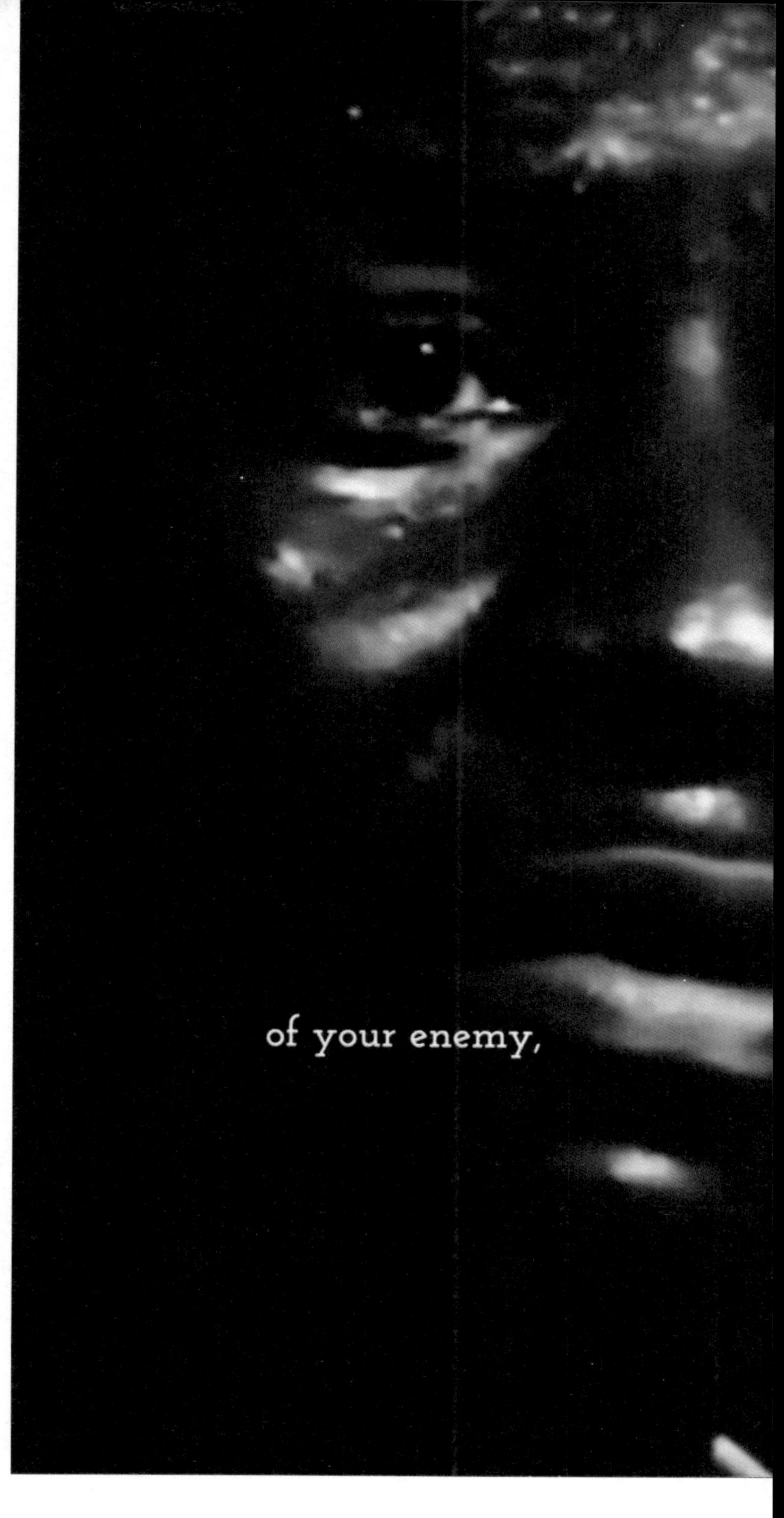

Screenshot from White's iPhone (May 2024) / Screenshot dall'iPhone di White (maggio 2024)

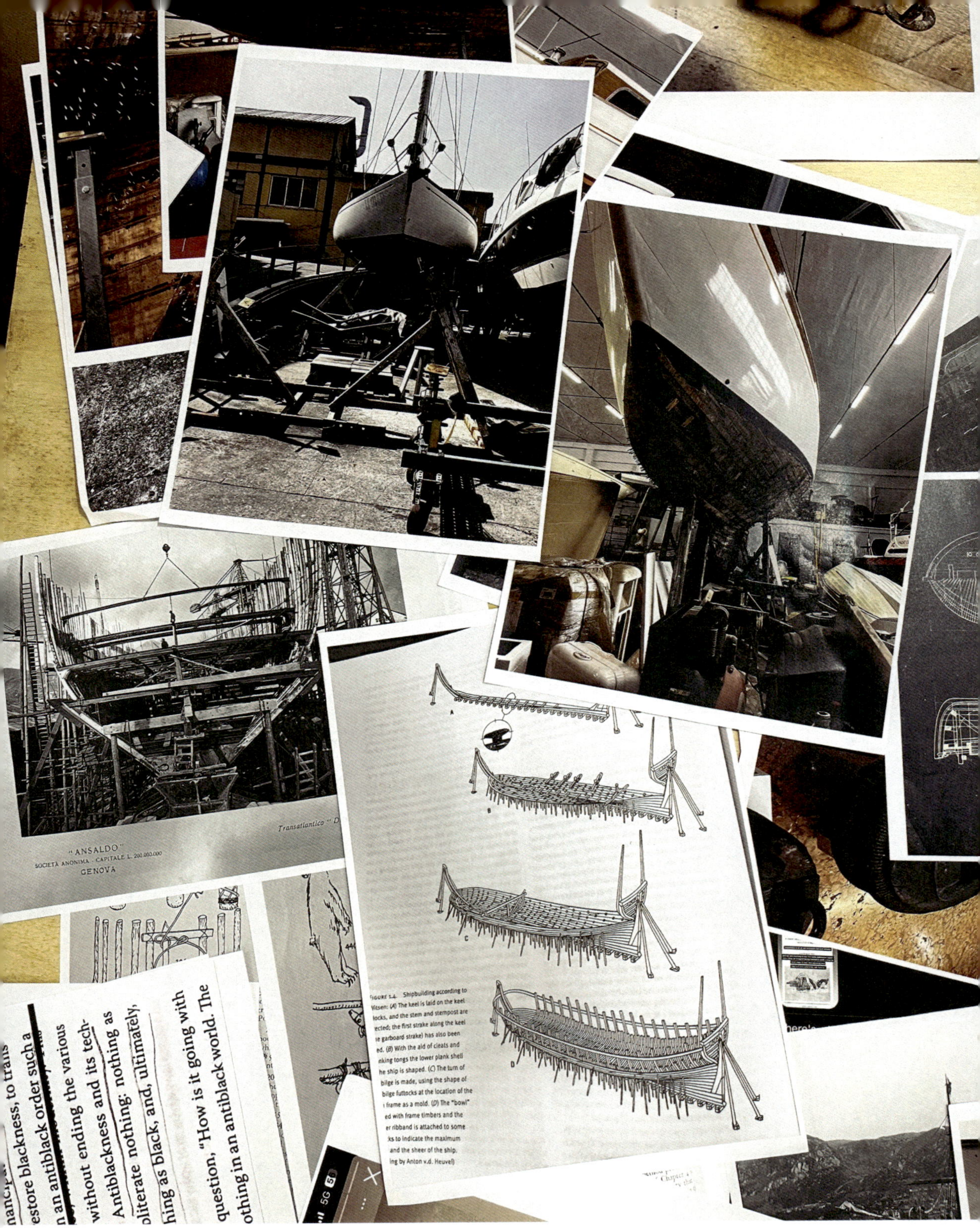

Reference images in White's studio (September 2023)
Foto di riferimento nello studio di White (settembre 2023)

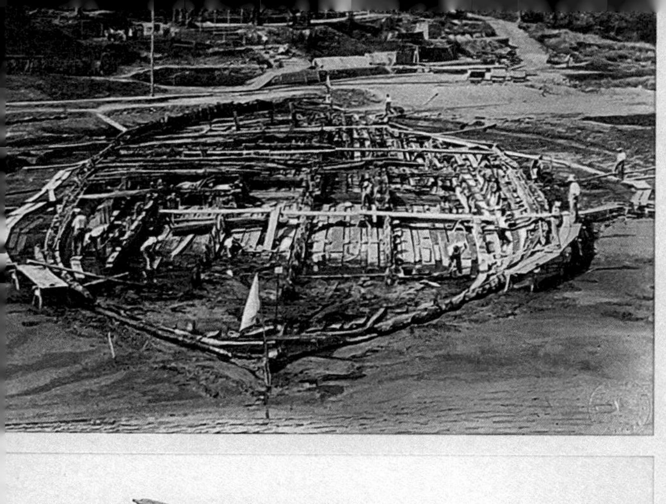

La prima nave emersa completamente (da G. Ucelli).
The first ship partially emerged. (from Ucelli's Archive).

La costruzione dell' hangar per ricoverare la prima nave (da G. Ucelli).
The hangar construction for the first ship recovering (from G. Ucelli).

L'alaggio della prima nave realizzato nell'Ottobre 1929 (da G. Ucelli).
The first ship slipways realized in October 1929 (from G. Ucelli).

La prima nave parzialmente emersa (dall' Archivio Ucelli).
The first ship partially emerged. (from Ucelli's Archive).

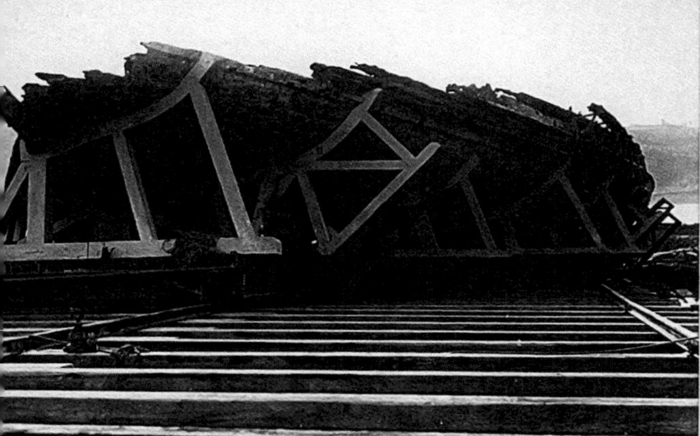

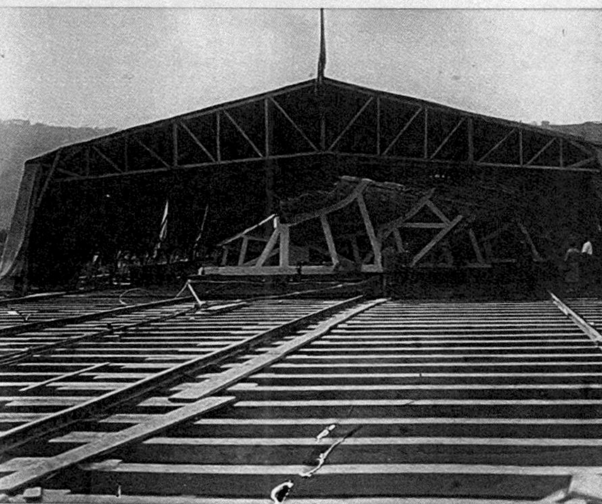

La prima nave emersa completamente (da G. Ucelli).
The first ship partially emerged. (from Ucelli's Archive).

La costruzione dell' hangar per ricoverare la prima nave (da G. Ucelli).
The hangar construction for the first ship recovering (from G. Ucelli).

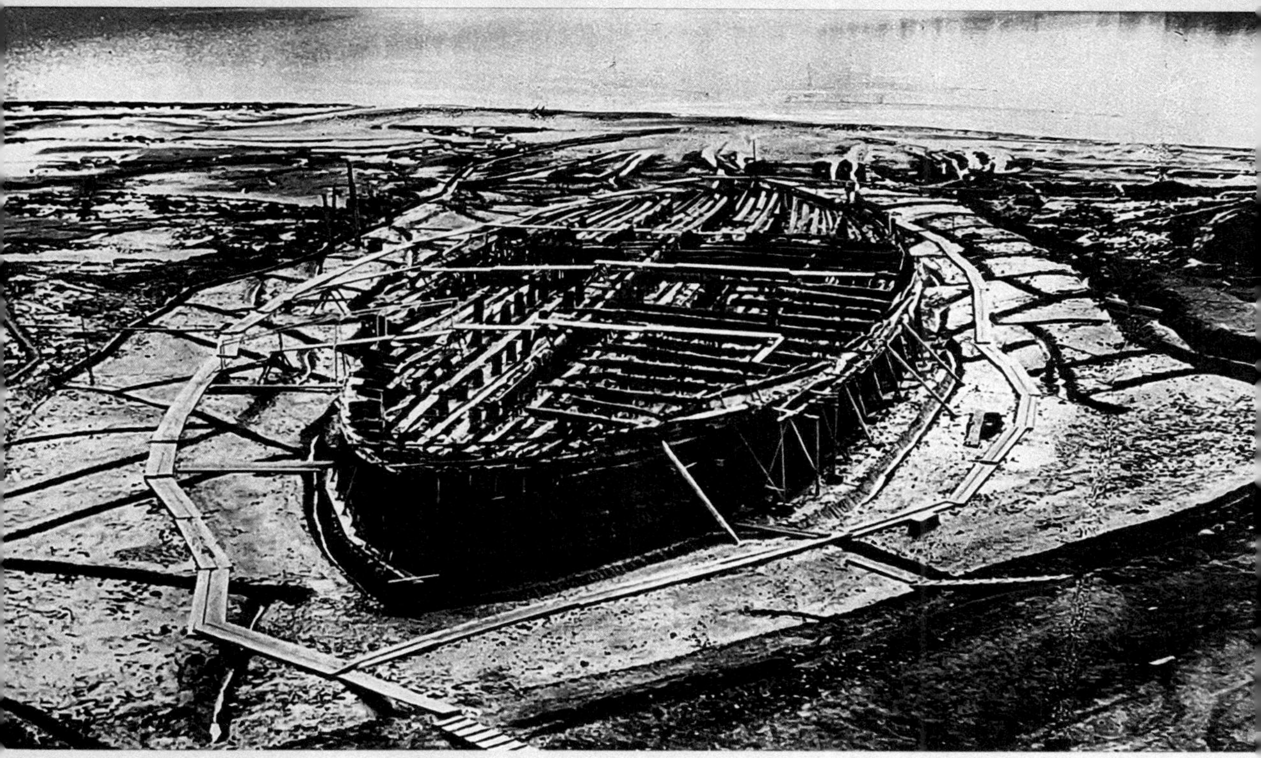

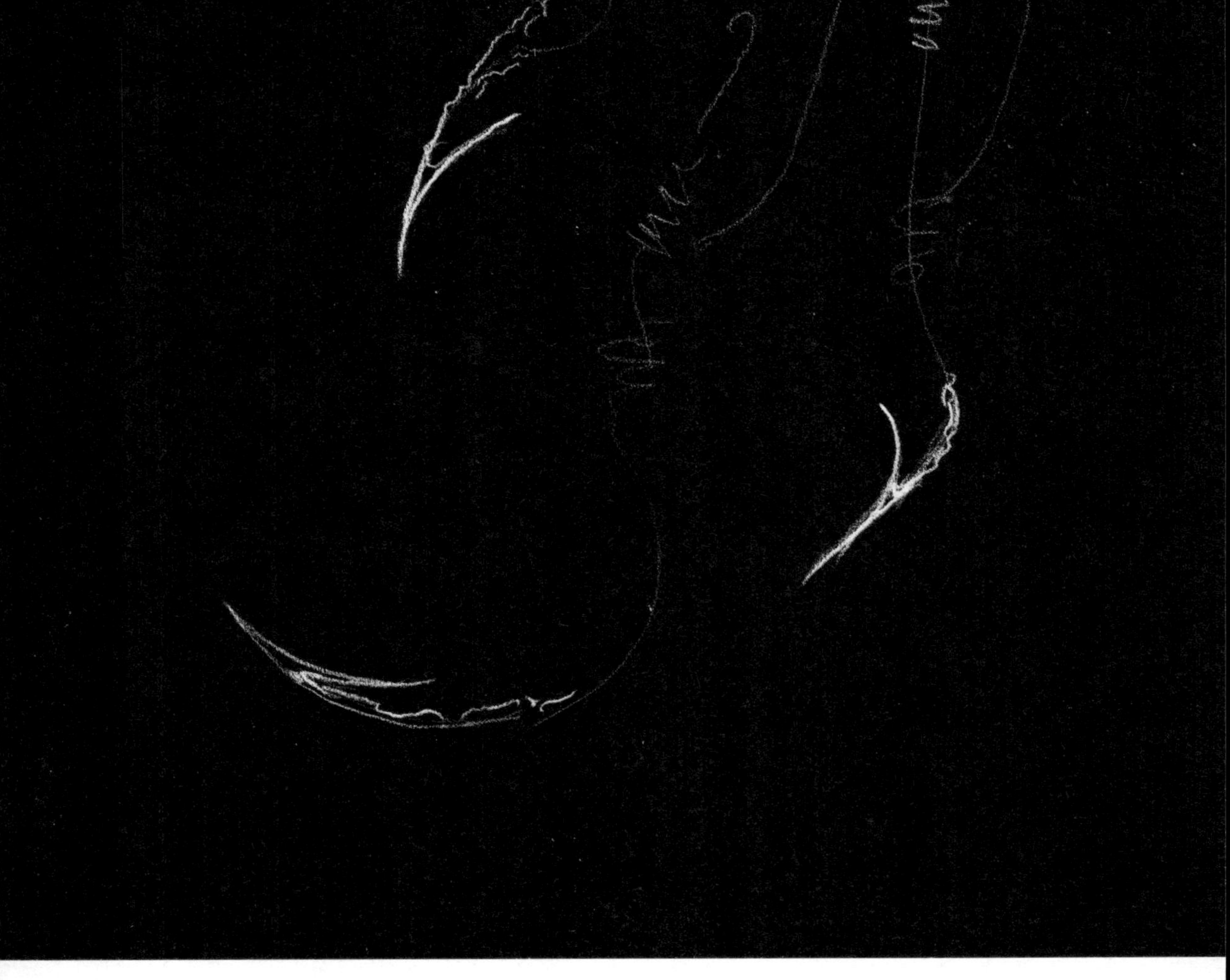

Preparatory sketch for / Disegno preparatorio di
the Collapsed, the Overthrown, yet ever insatiable (2022). Dominique White

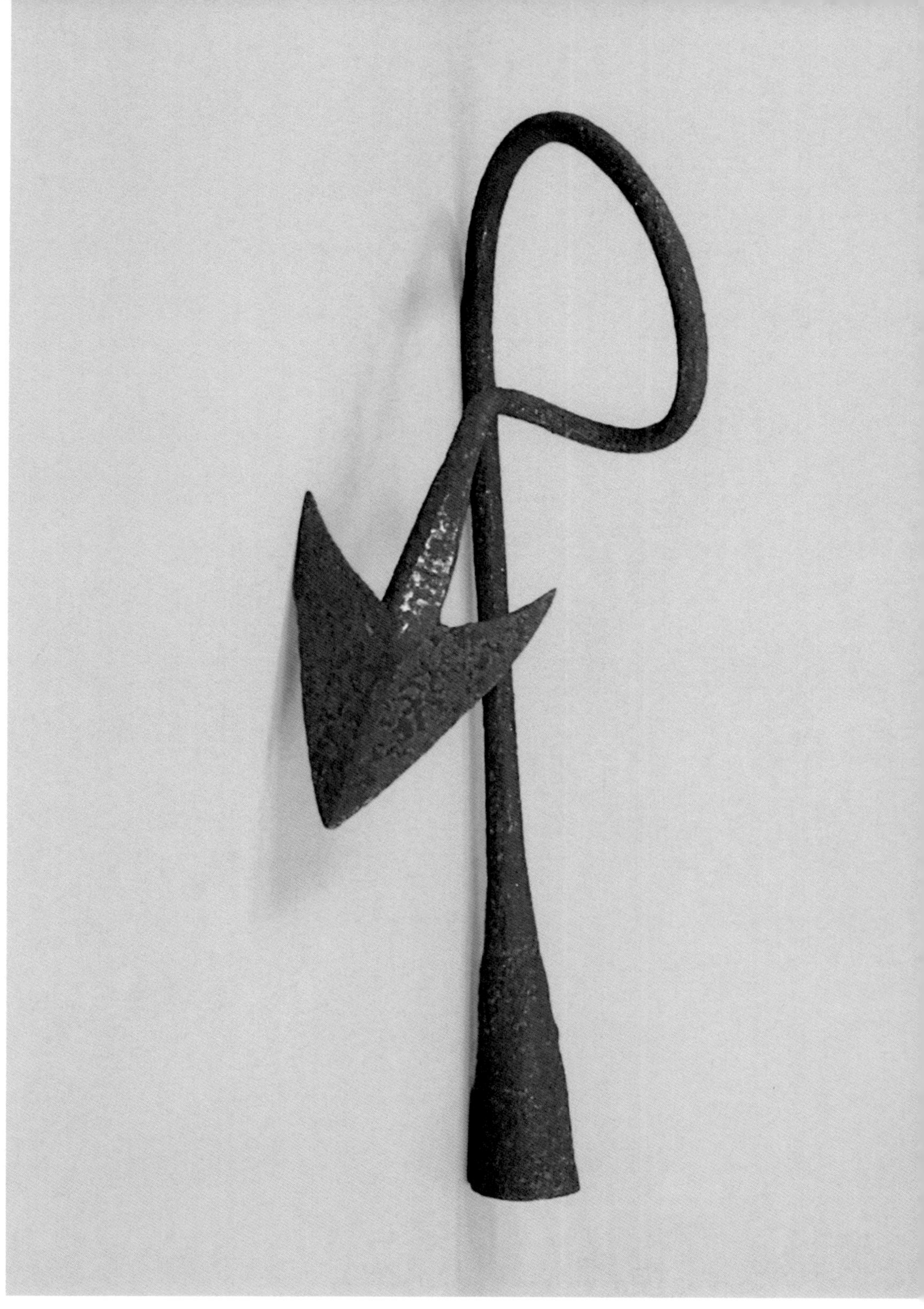

Reference image, source unknown / Immagine di riferimento, fonte sconosciuta

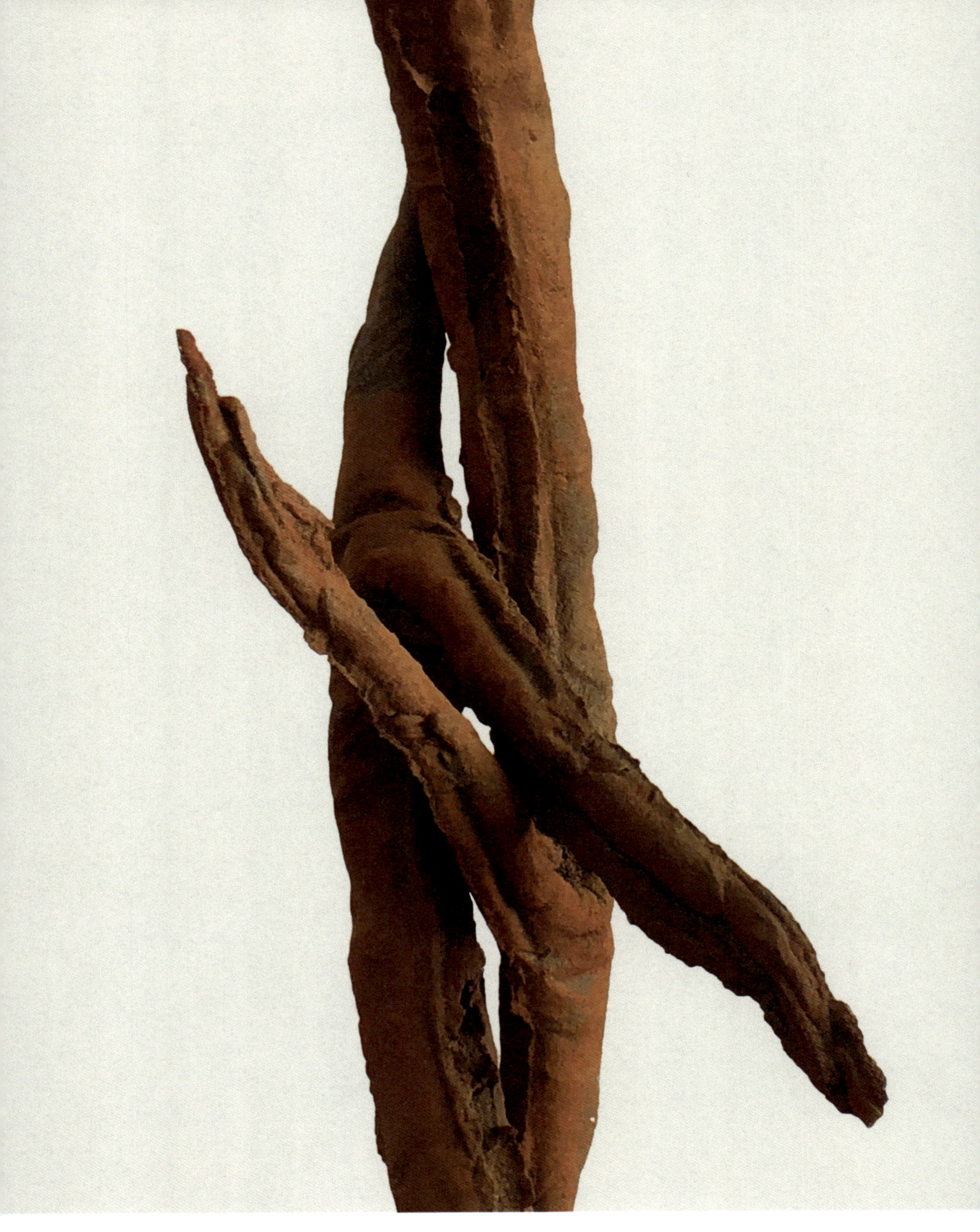

Detail of / Dettaglio di *Redemption*. Dominique White (March / marzo 2022)

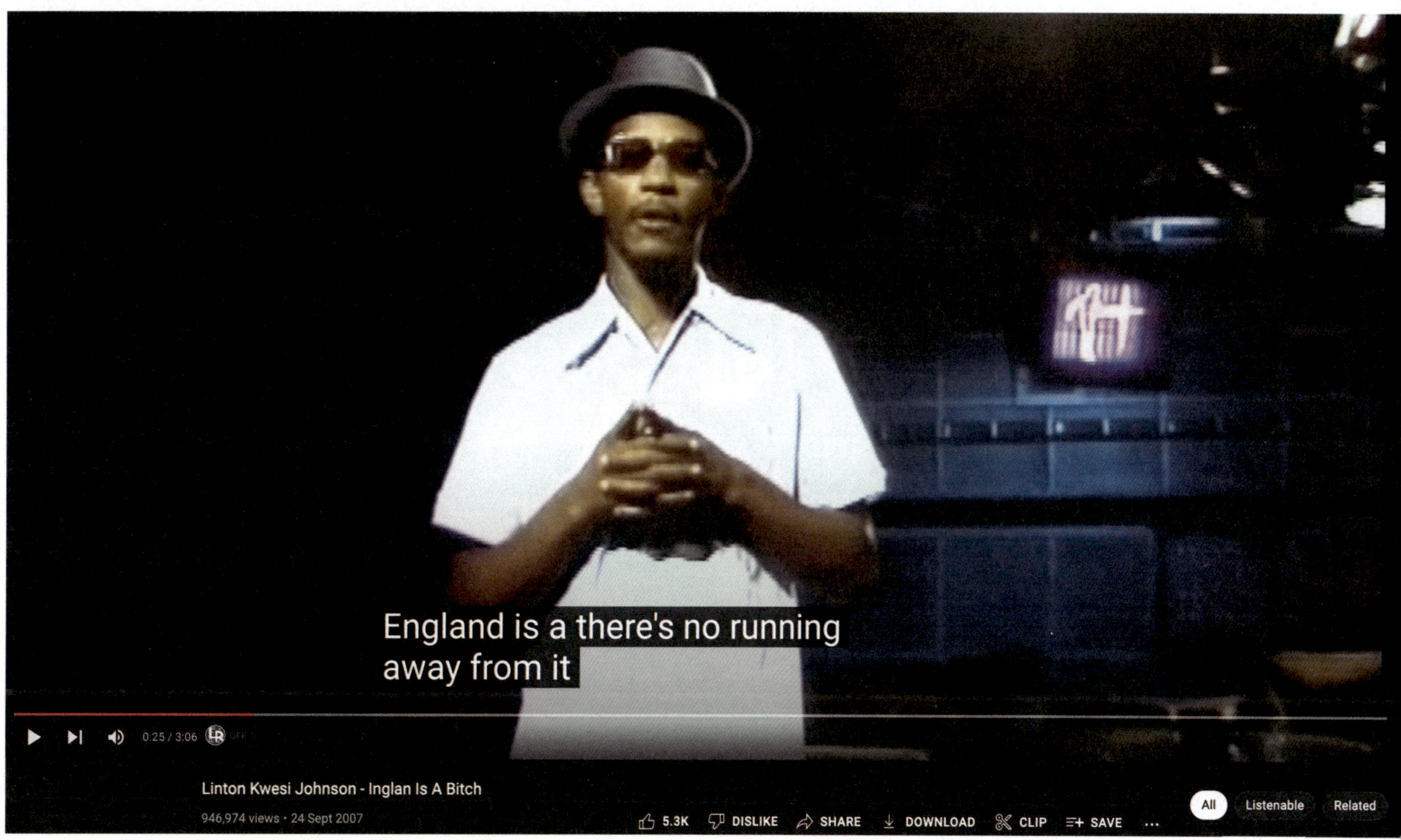

Screenshot from White's computer (March 2021) / Screenshot dal computer di White (marzo 2021)

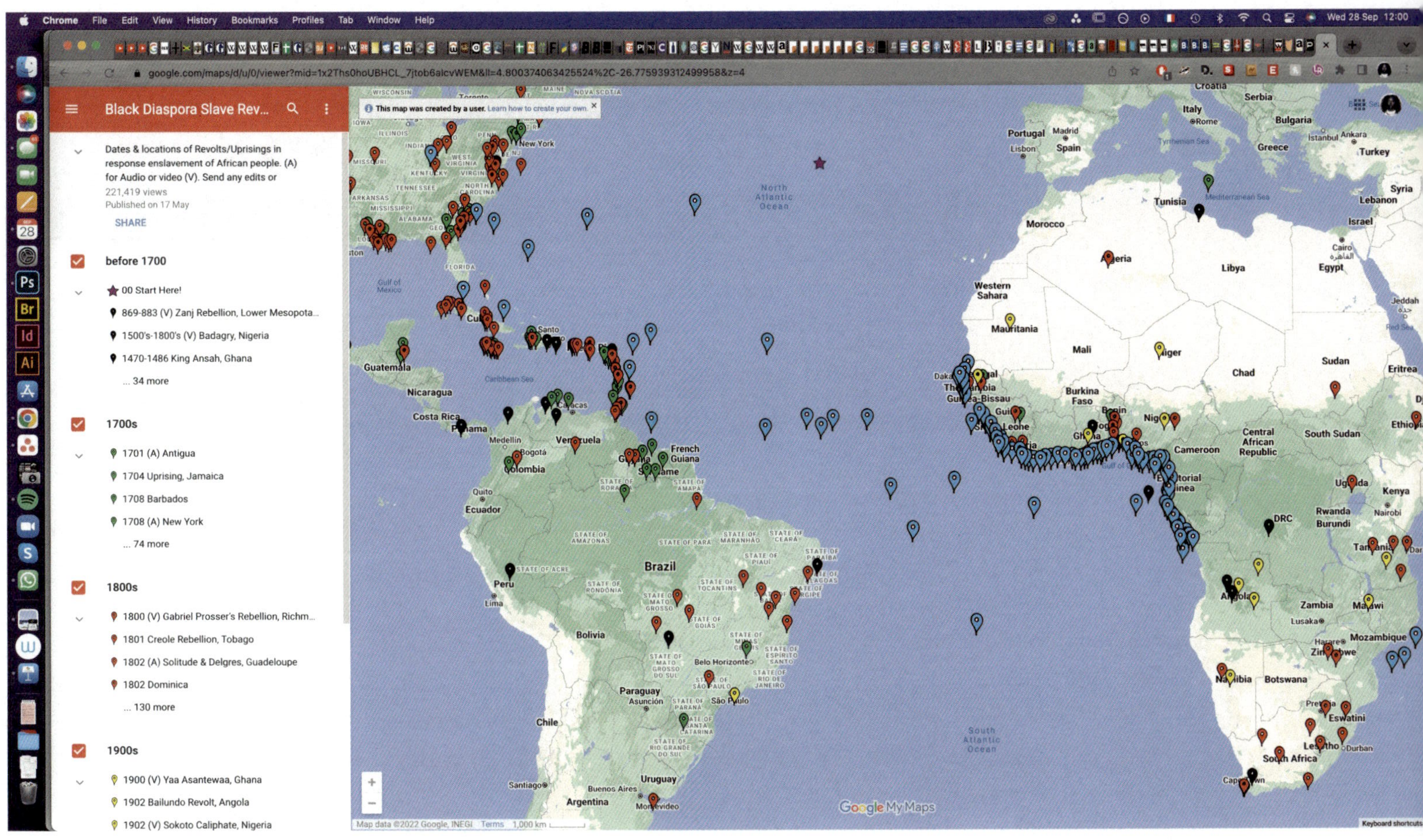

Screenshot from White's computer (September 2020)
Screenshot dal computer di White (settembre 2020)

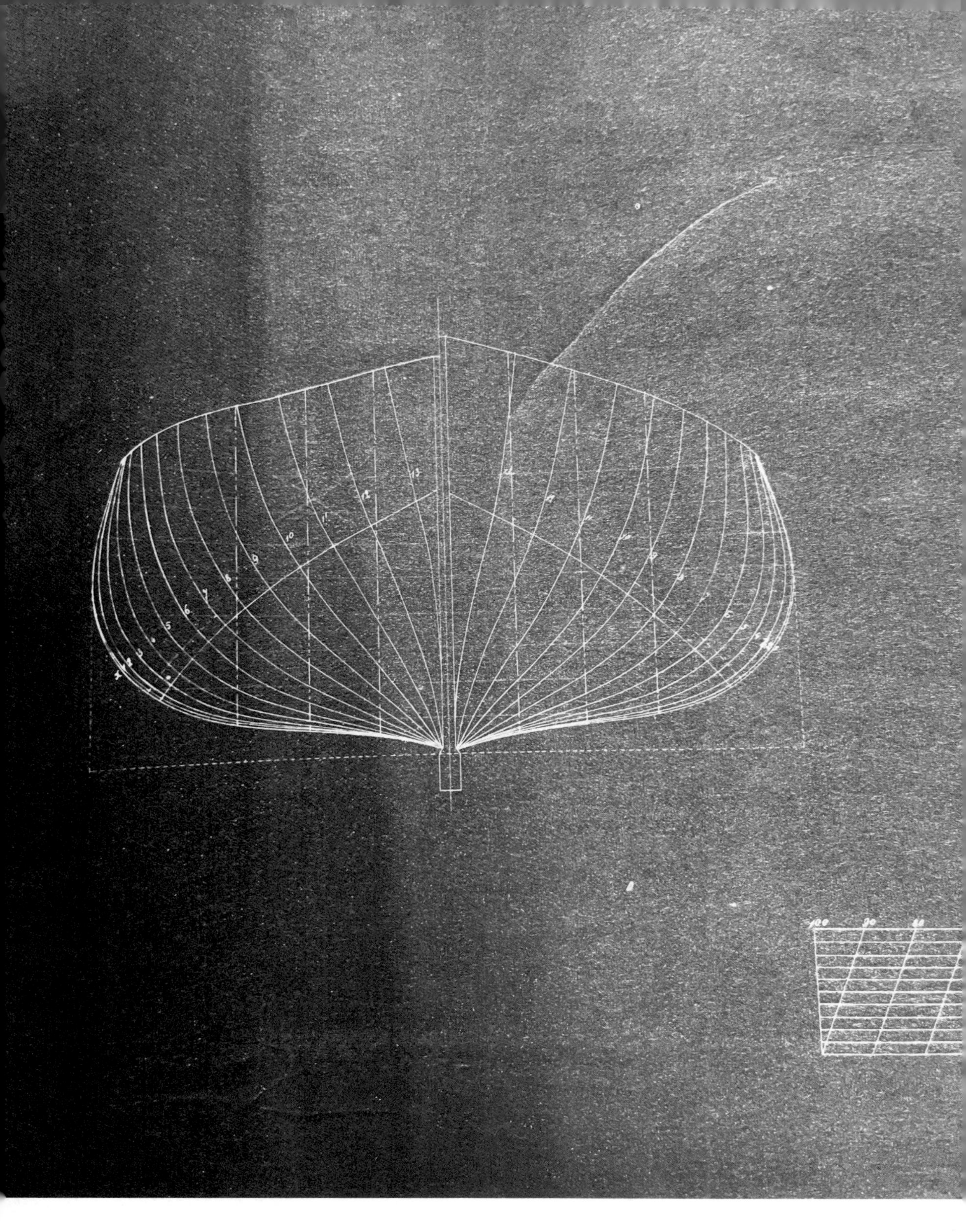

Scan of a blueprint in Genoa University's archives (June 2023)
Scansione di un progetto negli archivi dell'Università di Genova (giugno 2023)

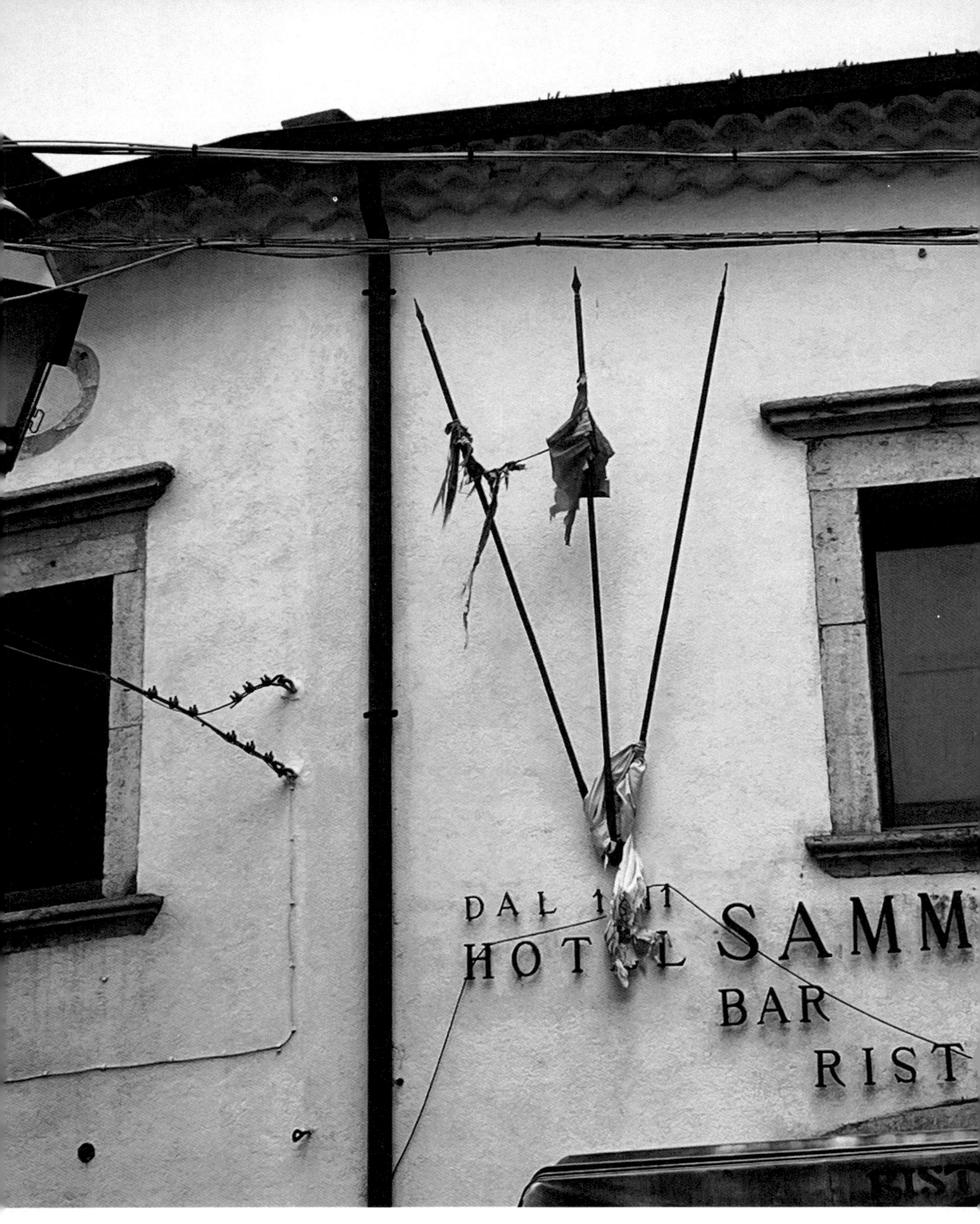

Neglected flagpoles in Agnone, Italy (May 2023)
Aste portabandiera abbandonate ad Agnone, Italia (maggio 2023)

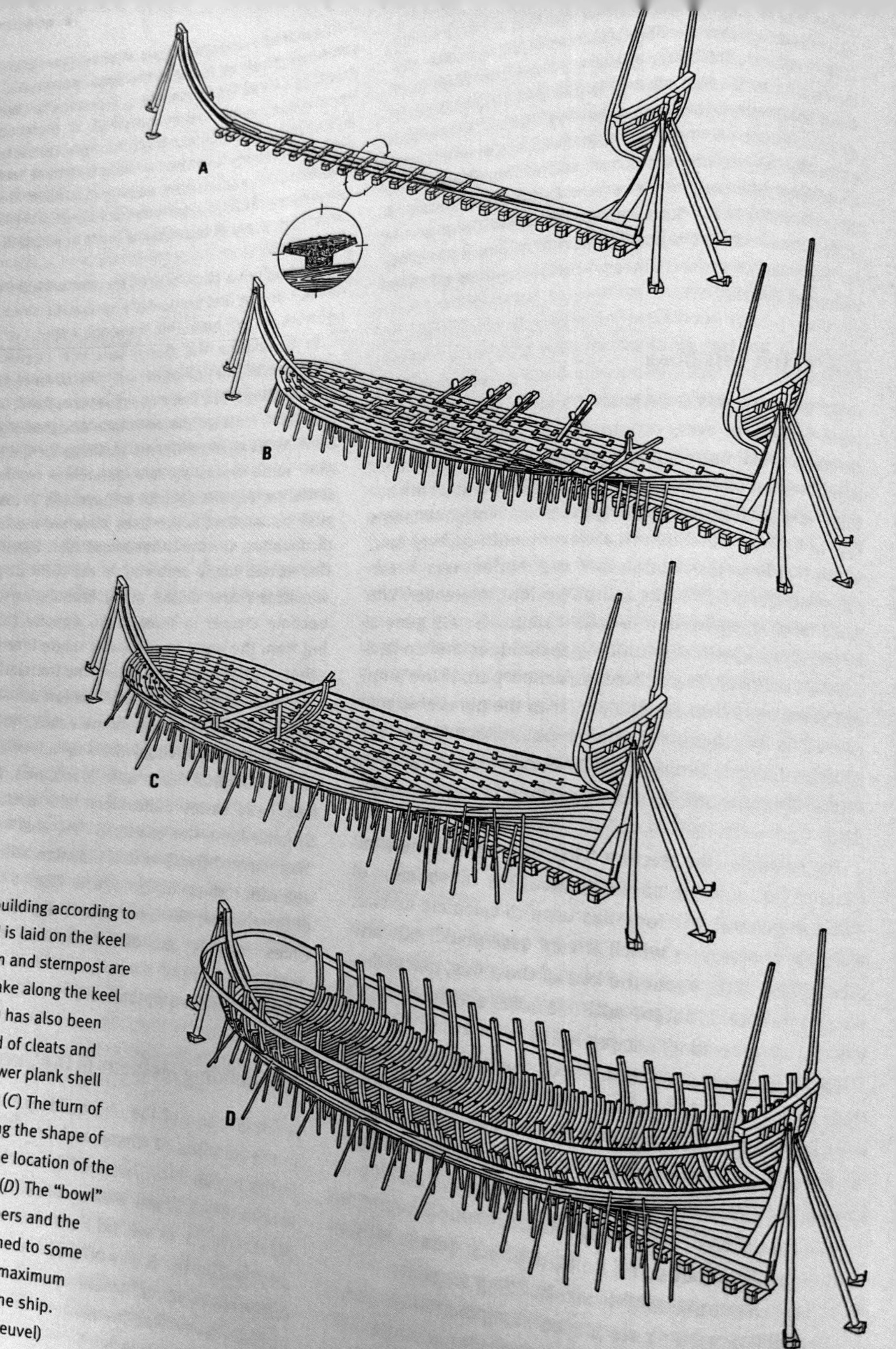

4. Shipbuilding according to
) The keel is laid on the keel
d the stem and sternpost are
e first strake along the keel
rd strake) has also been
ith the aid of cleats and
gs the lower plank shell
s shaped. (*C*) The turn of
ade, using the shape of
ocks at the location of the
s a mold. (*D*) The "bowl"
rame timbers and the
d is attached to some
icate the maximum
sheer of the ship.
ton v.d. Heuvel)

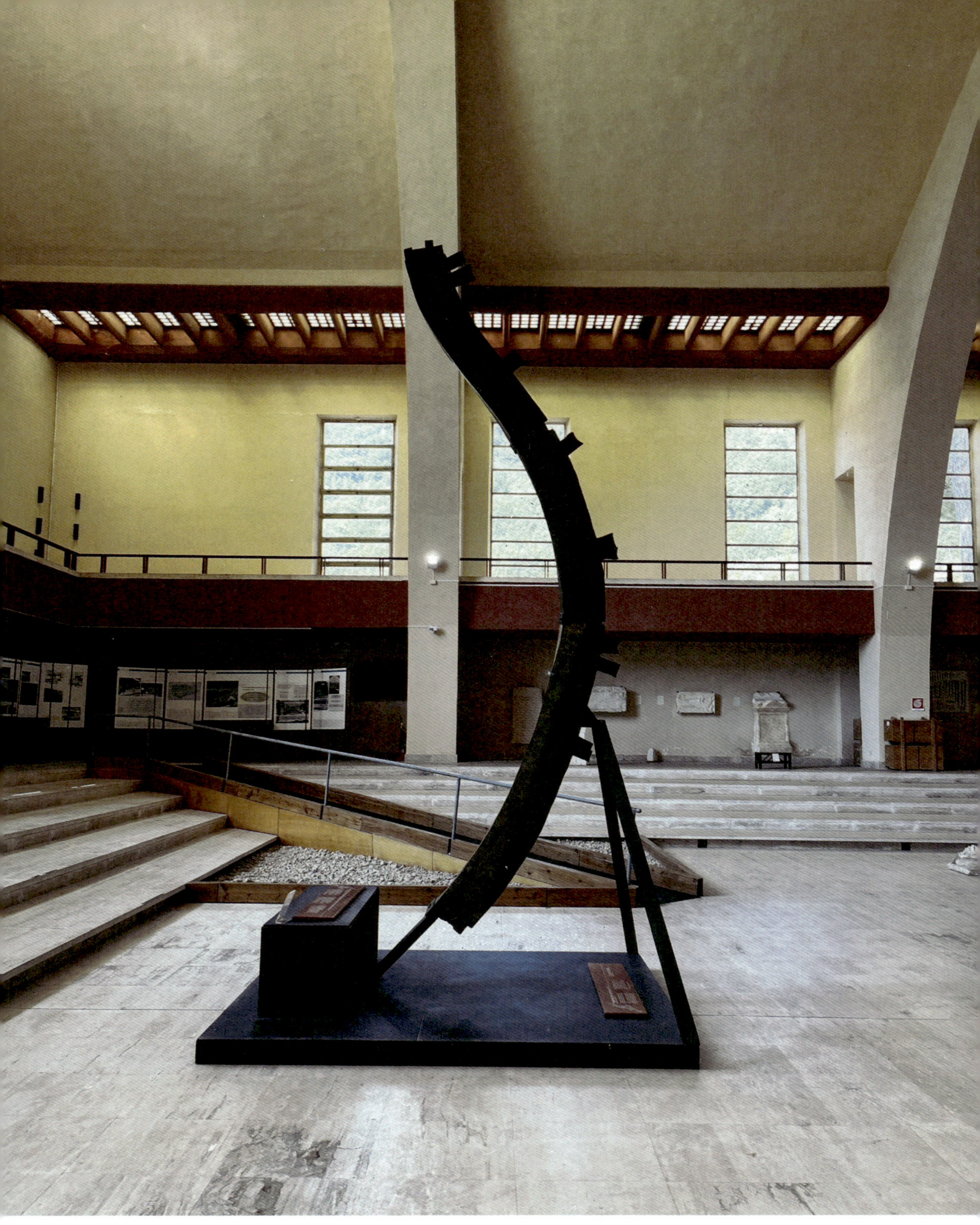

Photo taken in / Foto scattata al Museo delle Navi Romane (Italy, August / Italia, agosto 2023)

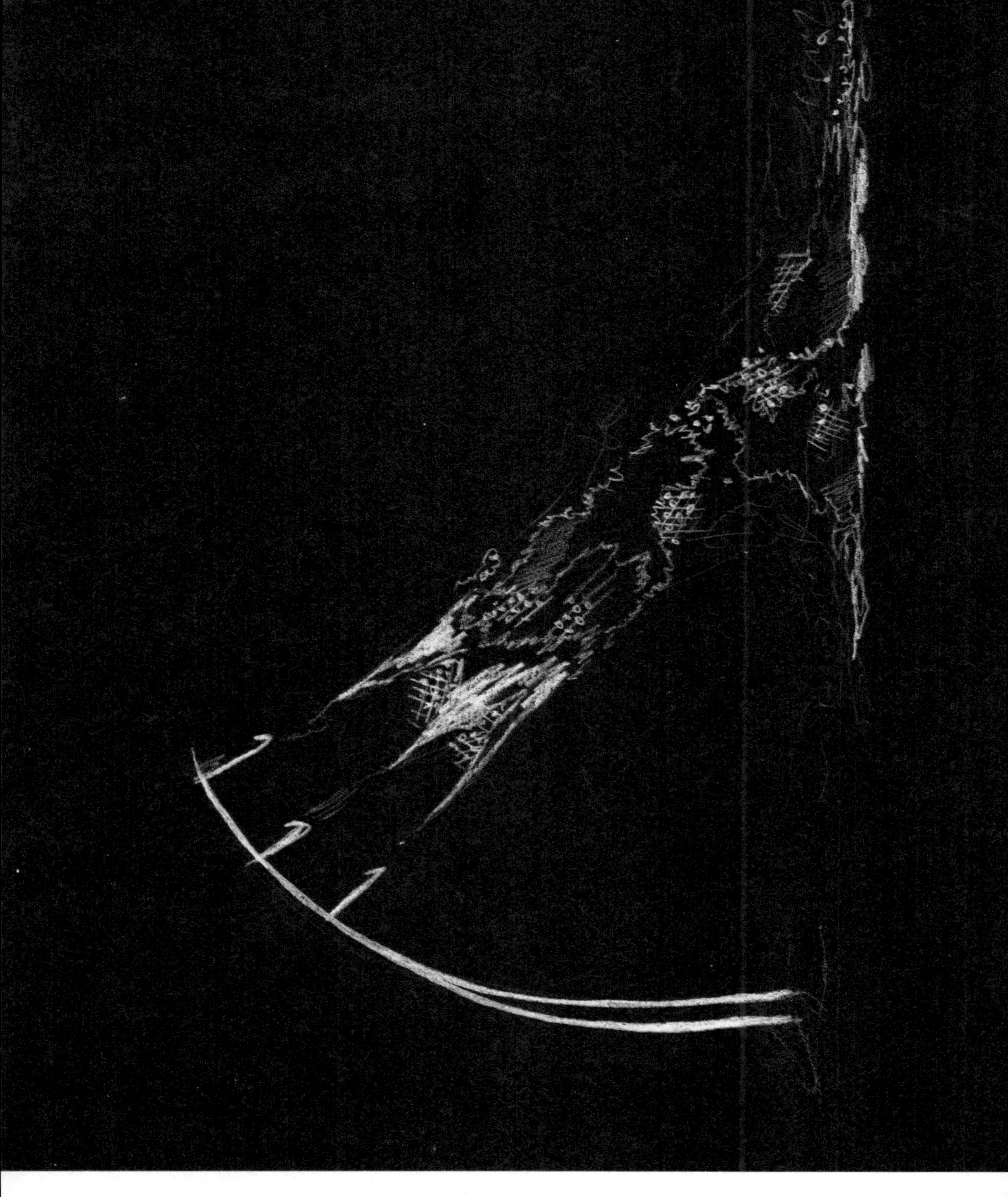

Preparatory sketch of / Disegno preparatorio di
Zero is My Country (2021). Dominique White (Chile, February / Cile, febbraio 2020)

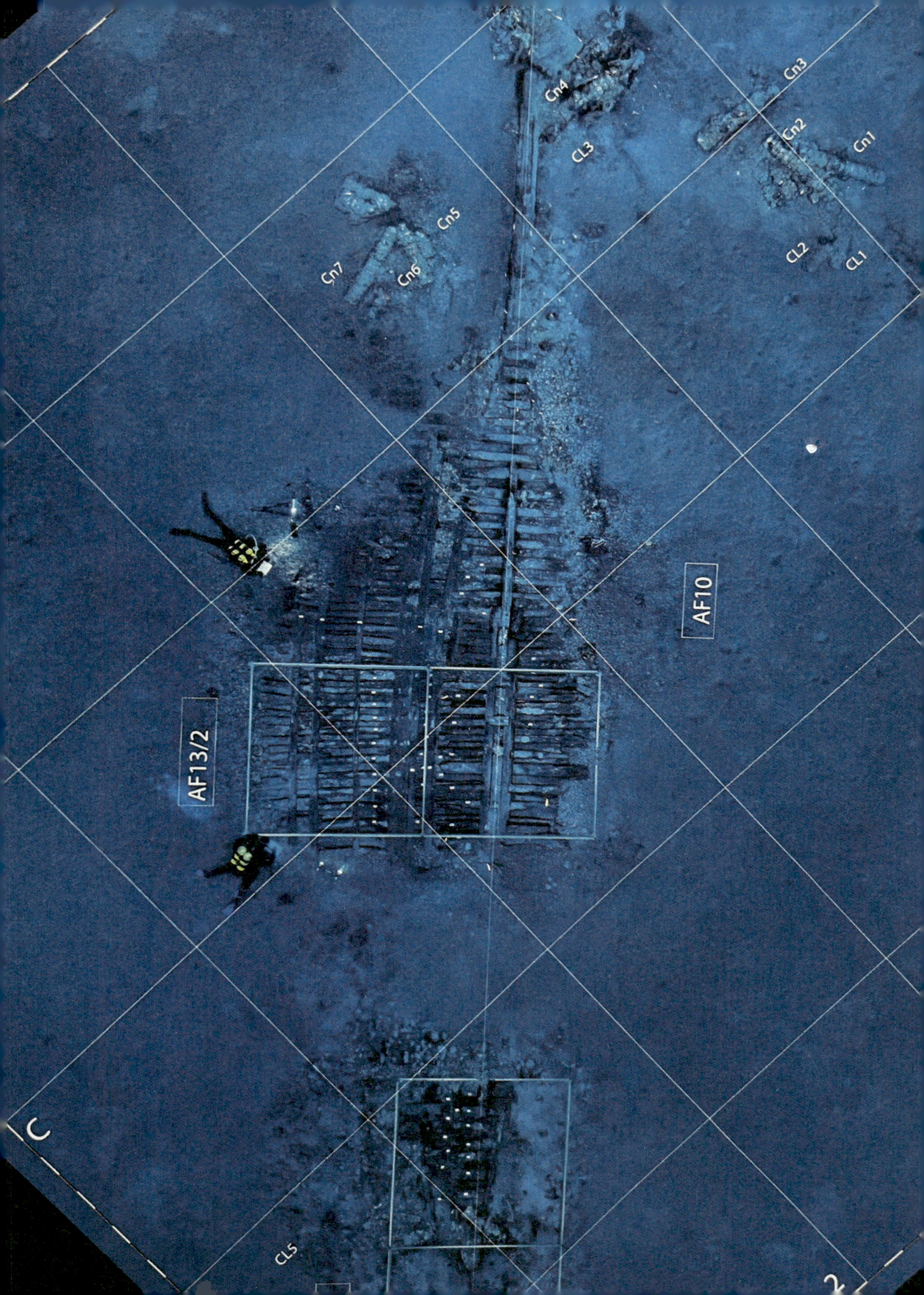

Cn4
Cn3
CL3
Cn2
Cn1
Cn5
CL2
CL1
Cn7
Cn6
AF10
AF13/2
C
CL5
2

KNOW YOUR OWN SHIP.

CHAPTER I.

DISPLACEMENT AND DEADWEIGHT.

CONTENTS.—What Displacement Means—The Relation of Weight and Displacement of a Floating Body—Displacement Curves, Construction and Uses—Deadweight Scales—"Tons per Inch" Immersion—Rule for "Tons per Inch"—Curve of "Tons per Inch"—Illustration of the Use of "Tons per Inch" Curve—Ship Passing from River to Sea Water—Density of Water—Use of Hydrometer—Precautions against Overloading—Coefficient of Displacement—Some Examples—Rule for Coefficient of Fineness.

Terms.—"Displacement," "Deadweight," and "Tonnage" are terms often heard and used by those associated with ships and shipping in some form or other, but are not always definitely understood. They are, however, easy of explanation, and we shall, at the outset, devote our attention briefly to the two former—Displacement and Deadweight. The last—Tonnage—being a subject of larger dimensions, though simple in its character—will be reserved for a later chapter.

Displacement.—Any body floating in a fluid displaces or dislodges a certain volume of that fluid, and the weight of the displaced fluid is equal to the weight of the floating body. This is the first law of Hydrostatics.

Displacement, in the technical sense as applied to ships, or other floating bodies, refers to the displacement of the water effected in obedience to the above law. The quantity of water displaced, expressed as a rule in cubic feet, is called the volume of displacement, and the corresponding weight displaced is termed the weight of *Displacement*, and is usually given in tons.

That the weight of a floating body is equal to the weight of displacement may be demonstrated by a simple experiment, viz.

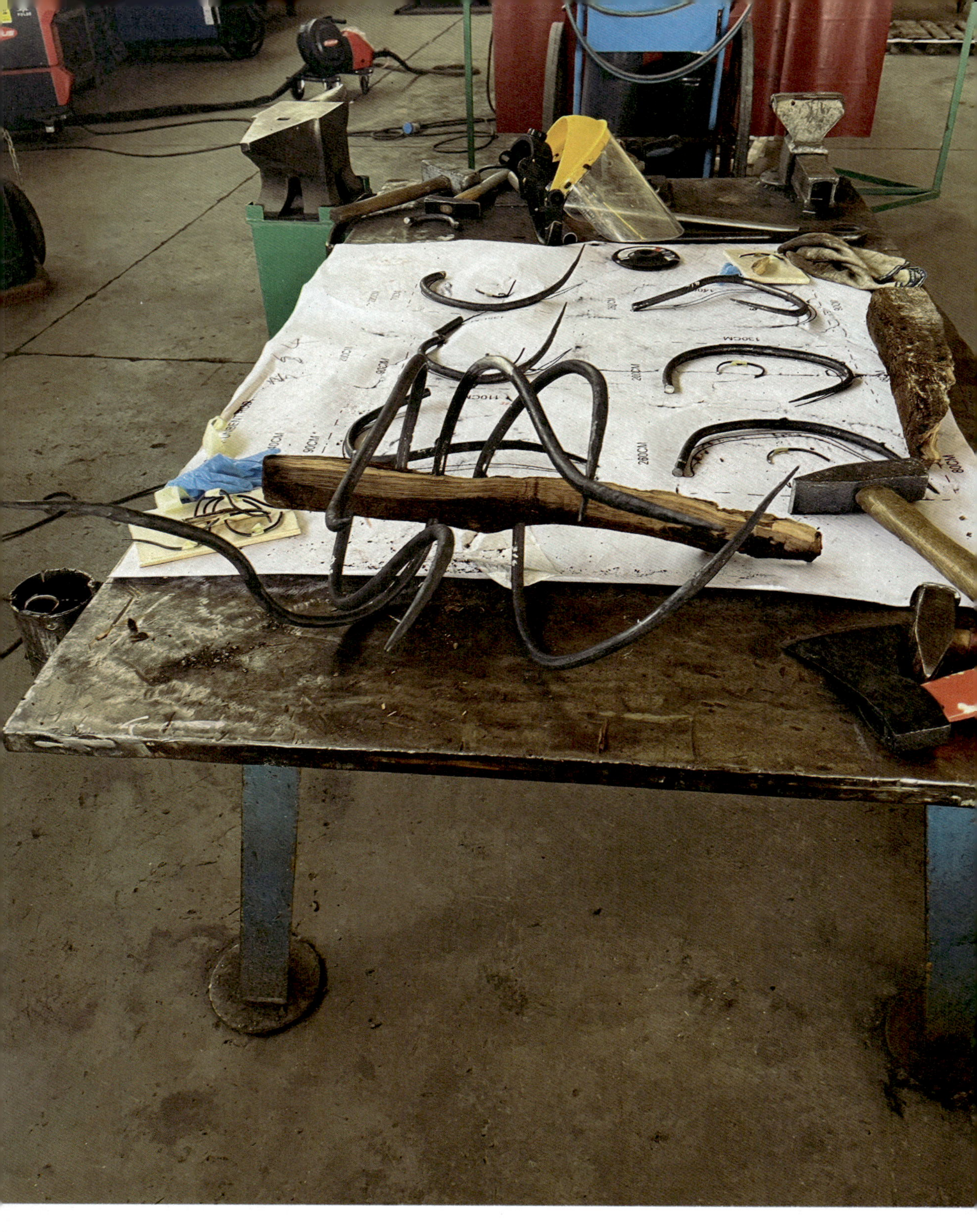

Preparatory model for / Modello preparatorio per *Deadweight* (Italy, October / Italia, ottobre 2023)

I MUST BECOME A MENACE
TO MY ENEMIES

Dedicated to the Poet Agostinho Neto,
President of The People's Republic of Angola: 1976

1

I will no longer lightly walk behind
a one of you who fear me:
                              Be afraid.
I plan to give you reasons for your jumpy fits
And facial tics
I will not walk politely on the pavements anymore
And this is dedicated in particular
To those who fear my footsteps
Or the insubstantial rattling of my grocery
cart
then turn around
see me
and hurry on
away from this impressive terror I must be:
I plan to blossom bloody on an afternoon
surrounded by my comrades singing
terrible revenge in merciless
accelerating
rhythms

JUNE JORDAN

But
I have watched a blind man studying his face.
I have set the table in the evening and sat down
to eat the news.
Regularly
I have gone to sleep.
There is no one to forgive me.
The dead do not give a damn.
I live like a lover
who drops her dime into the phone
just as the subway shakes into the station
wasting her message
canceling the question of her call:

fulminating or forgetful but late
and always after the fact that could save or
condemn me

I must become the action of my fate.

2

How many of my brothers and my sisters
will they kill
before I teach myself
retaliation?
Shall we pick a number?
South Africa for instance:
do we agree that more than ten thousand
in less than a year but that less than
five thousand slaughtered in more than six
months will
WHAT IS THE MATTER WITH ME?

I must become a menace to my enemies

3

And if I
if I ever let you slide
who should be extirpated from my universe
who should be cauterized from earth
completely
(lawandorder jerkoffs of the first the
terrorist degree)
then let my body fail my soul
in its bedeviled lecheries

And if I
if I ever let love go
because the hatred and the whisperings
become a phantom dictate I o-
bey in lieu of impulse and realities
(the blossoming flamingos of my
wild mimosa trees)
then let love freeze me
out.

I must become
I must become a menace to my enemies.

THE ATTEMPT

IL TENTATIVO

OLAMIJU FAJEMISIN

1 Hannah Black, 'Fractal Freedoms', *Afterall: A Journal of Art, Context and Enquiry*, vol. 41 (Spring–Summer 2016) 8.

2 Rev & Reve, 'Joy James: Fear Factor, Quantum Entanglement, and Revolutionary Love' (21 June 2023) (youtube.com/watch?v=z3-mCUZnlJY).

3 Ibid.

4 Ibid.

5 'Ima-Abasi Okon in conversation with Taylor Le Melle', *CURA*, no. 33 (Spring 2020) (curamagazine.com/digital/ima-abasi-okon).

6 Patrice Douglass, Selamawit D. Terrefe and Frank B. Wilderson III, 'Afro-Pessimism', in African American Studies, Oxford Bibliographies (28 August 2018) (oxfordbibliographies.com/view/document/obo-9780190280024/obo-9780190280024-0056.xml).

'If freedom and slavery [...] are locked in a fatal mutual interdependence, what is the synthesis or the knife that cuts through?'[1] Hannah Black

'I don't have answers, I just raise questions.'[2] Joy James

It tickles me whenever an artist or theorist who is demonstrably working through an Afropessimist lens of interpretation refuses to identify with – let alone be named in the same sentence as – the theory. It happens a lot. Rarely are such cases self-aware.

The political philosopher and writer Joy James, for one, speaking informally towards the end of a recent talk, 'Fear Factor, Quantum Entanglement, and Revolutionary Love' (2023), confesses how she finds it 'ironic' how everyone hates the Afropessimists, when they are the 'most intelligible'; that she has found 'no language [...] competent to address' certain paradigms besides Afropessimism, the theory which prescribes an understanding of humanity as predicated on antiblackness; but that ultimately, she is not an Afropessimist, and 'they keep telling [her] to stop saying [she's] not, but anyway…'.[3] When there is something 'to lose', there can be nothing to lose: 'You cannot "articulate" and keep your job, or keep your money, or host your conferences, or not be shamed, or humiliated, or tracked, or surveilled – if you "go rogue", that means to go outside the discourse.'[4]

The prohibiting failure of language necessitates the enaction of a gesture through which to speak. In a conversation between writer Taylor Le Melle and artist Ima-Abasi Okon, the latter ruminates over the abstract concept of 'the attempt', describing 'an aspiration [...] the space between [identifying] the desire and achieving the desire, and the mechanism that allows you to get closer to it'.[5] The attempt is what facilitates catalysis. The attempt is kinetically charged, wanton, boundlessly creative. An uninhibited zone. The attempt lingers long after it is made. In the context of sculpture, the attempt is the gesture through which a work is wrought – the attempt is ignition, sinking, breaching, smelting, fusing, smiting. Marking the object as a body, relating it to property, is an attempt. Destruction is an attempt.

There is no interpersonal or institutional orientation towards Blackness, but Blackness is the essence of that which orients.[6] Since the security of our present reality depends on the anxiety caused by the very presence of Blackness (the white libidinal economy of antiblackness), strategies of black fungibility and fugitivity become necessary actions

“Se la libertà e la schiavitù […] sono legate in una fatale interdipendenza reciproca, qual è la sintesi o il coltello che le separa?”[1] Hannah Black

“Non ho risposte, sollevo solo domande”[2] Joy James

Ogni volta mi diverte il fatto che un artista o un teorico, che ragiona attraverso una lente afropessimista, si rifiuti di identificarsi – e tanto meno di essere nominato nella stessa frase – con la teoria. Succede spesso, ma raramente se ne è coscienti.

La filosofa politica e scrittrice Joy James, per esempio, parlando informalmente verso la fine di una recente conferenza intitolata: “Fear Factor, Quantum Entanglement, and Revolutionary Love” (2023), confessa di trovare “ironico” il fatto che tutti odino gli afropessimisti, anche quando sono loro i “più intelligibili”; e dice di non aver trovato “nessun linguaggio […] adatto ad affrontare” alcuni paradigmi ad eccezione dell’afropessimismo, teoria che stabilisce una comprensione dell’umanità come predicata dalla afrofobia; ma che, in definitiva, lei non è un’afropessimista, e che “continuano a dirle di smettere di sostenere che non lo sia, ma comunque…”[3]. Quando c’è qualcosa “da perdere”, non ci può essere nulla da perdere: “Non si può ‘articolare un discorso’ e mantenere il proprio lavoro, o conservare i propri soldi, o tenere le proprie conferenze, o non essere imbarazzati, o umiliati, o seguiti, o sorvegliati – se si ‘diventa disonesti’, il che significa uscire dal discorso”[4].

Il fallimento proibitivo del linguaggio richiede di comunicare in altro modo. In una conversazione tra la scrittrice Taylor Le Melle e l’artista Ima-Abasi Okon, quest’ultima si sofferma sul concetto astratto di “tentativo”, descrivendo “un’aspirazione […] lo spazio tra [l’identificazione] del desiderio e il raggiungimento del desiderio, e il meccanismo che permette di avvicinarsi ad esso”[5]. Il tentativo è ciò che facilita la catalisi. Il tentativo è cineticamente carico, volubile, smisuratamente creativo. Una zona disinibita. Il tentativo permane a lungo dopo la sua realizzazione. Nel contesto della scultura, il tentativo è il gesto attraverso il quale si realizza un’opera – il tentativo è accensione, affondamento, sfondamento, separazione, fusione, attrazione. Marcare l’oggetto come corpo, metterlo in relazione con la proprietà, è un tentativo. La distruzione è un tentativo.

Non esiste un orientamento interpersonale o istituzionale verso la “Blackness”, ma la “Blackness” è l’essenza di ciò che orienta[6]. Poiché la sicurezza della nostra realtà attuale dipende dall’ansia causata dalla presenza stessa della “Blackness” (l’economia lasciva bianca della

1 Hannah Black, ‘Fractal Freedoms’, *Afterall: A Journal of Art, Context and Enquiry*, Vol.41 (primavera/estate 2016) p.8. Se non diversamente specificato, la traduzione in italiano dei testi originali è curata dalla traduttrice.
2 Rev & Reve, ‘Joy James: Fear Factor, Quantum Entanglement, and Revolutionary Love’ (21 giugno 2023) (youtube.com/watch?v=z3-mCUZnlJY).
3 Ibid.
4 Ibid.
5 Ima-Abasi Okon in conversazione con Taylor Le Melle’, *CURA* No.33 (primavera 2020).
6 Patrice Douglass, Selamawit D. Terrefe, Frank B. Wilderson III, ‘Afro-Pessimismo’, in African American Studies, Oxford Bibliographies (28 agosto 2018) (oxfordbibliographies.com/view/document/obo-9780190280024/obo-9780190280024-0056.xml).

to divert and absorb this white libido. Black errancy equals resistance to peaceful coexistence. An attempt.

To frame her riverlike essay 'Fractal Freedoms' (2016) – which dives off from Paul Gilroy's description of the transfer of black cultural forms (of human survival) across the black Atlantic as "fractal" in the sense of a complex geometric pattern, in which the minor details of its structure viewed at any scale repeat elements of the overall pattern – artist and writer Hannah Black provides the example of 'the art historical rupture of [Kazimir Malevich's] *Black Square* [1915]'.[7] Once so confidently heralded by the artist as a 'refuge in the form of the square', and a bid 'desperately to free art from the dead weight of the real world', the sovereignty of the black square as a zero-point of representation and site of, at least perceived, neutrality, has been violently upended.[8] In 2015, conservators at the Tretyakov Gallery in Moscow discovered the remains of a Cyrillic hand inscription translatable as 'battle of the negroes' – hardly a non sequitur – legible through composited X-rays of the layers of paint and varnish. The joke is an overt reference to a late nineteenth-century single-panel comic by Frenchman Alphonse Allais that depicts an elaborately bordered swathe of solid black nothing, captioned: 'Combat de Nègres dans une cave pendant la nuit' ('Negros fighting in a cave at night').[9]

The reduction of Malevich's grand gesture to an antiblack one-liner demonstrates, per Black, the accident of how 'in light of the joke about darkness, negation itself becomes representation; what is represented is the nothingness of certain subjects, which indicates a certain nothingness in subjectivity itself'. Double entendres abound; the admittedly 'complicated' language attempts to convey the significance of the revelation of this work as hinging on the racist punchline that forms the not-so 'secret infrastructure of the modern subject'.[10] Brimming with perceived hubris, Tretyakov staffers were proud to exhibit these findings as part of the work's centenary exhibition, going on record to cite the evidence of the scrawling as proof that the artist had not simply 'grabbed a canvas and quickly painted the *Black Square*', calling into question not the globally endemic condition of antiblackness, or Malevich's fetishistic need to conceal, and thus prescribe, the invisibility of Blackness – literally, *painting over* signifier and subject – but the right of elapsed time as a means of critical interrogation; the right to conceptual and ontological decay; the right of curiosity to kill cats; the right of a work's history to fall apart; and the right of a work to similarly dematerialise. A resized digital reproduction of the square used to illustrate Black's text flatly represents its state of disrepair: patchy and

7 Black, op. cit., 6.

8 Ibid.

9 Sophia Kishkovsky, 'There is more to Malevich's *Black Square* than a hidden racist joke, Moscow curators reveal', *The Art Newspaper* (19 November 2015).

10 Black, op. cit., 8.

afrofobia), le strategie di sostituibilità e fragilità nera diventano azioni necessarie per deviare e assorbire questa libido bianca. L'erranza nera pone sullo stesso piano la resistenza e la coesistenza pacifica. Un tentativo.

Per inquadrare il suo saggio verboso, "Fractal Freedoms" (2016) – che prende le mosse dalla descrizione di Paul Gilroy del trasferimento di forme culturali nere (di sopravvivenza umana) attraverso l'Atlantico nero come "frattale", ovvero un complesso modello geometrico in cui i dettagli secondari della sua struttura, visti a qualsiasi scala, ripetono elementi del modello complessivo – l'artista e scrittrice Hannah Black fornisce l'esempio della "rottura storico-artistica del *Quadrato nero* [1915] di [Kazimir Malevich]"[7]. Una volta che l'artista aveva parlato con tanta sicurezza di un "rifugio nella forma del quadrato" e di un tentativo "disperato di liberare l'arte dal peso morto del mondo reale", la sovranità del quadrato nero come punto zero della rappresentazione e luogo di neutralità, per lo meno percepita, è stata violentemente stravolta[8]. Nel 2015 i restauratori della Galleria Tretyakov di Mosca hanno scoperto i resti di un'iscrizione a mano in cirillico, traducibile come "battaglia dei negri" – difficilmente un *non sequitur* – leggibile attraverso le radiografie degli strati di pittura e vernice. Lo scherzo è un palese riferimento a una vignetta di fine Ottocento del fumetto del francese Alphonse Allais, che presenta una striscia di nero pieno incorniciata e accompagnata dalla didascalia "Combat de Nègres dans une cave, pendant la nuit" ("Combattimento di negri in una grotta di notte")[9].

La riduzione dell'eclatante gesto di Malevich a una battuta anti-nera dimostra, secondo Black, la coincidenza per cui "alla luce della battuta sull'oscurità, la negazione stessa diventa rappresentazione; ciò che viene rappresentato è l'inesistenza di certi soggetti, che indica una certa inesistenza nella soggettività stessa". I doppi sensi abbondano; il linguaggio, certo "complicato", permette di trasmettere il significato della rivelazione di quest'opera in quanto imperniata sulla battuta razzista che costruisce la non così "segreta infrastruttura del soggetto moderno"[10]. Entusiasmati dall'arroganza percepita, i collaboratori della Tretyakov sono stati orgogliosi di esporre queste scoperte nell'ambito della mostra per il centenario dell'opera, citando l'evidenza degli scarabocchi come prova che l'artista non aveva semplicemente "preso una tela e dipinto rapidamente il *Quadrato nero*", chiamando in causa non la condizione endemica globale della afrofobia, o il bisogno feticistico di Malevich di nascondere, e quindi prescrivere, l'invisibilità della "Blackness" – letteralmente, *dipingendo sopra* il significante e il soggetto – ma il diritto del tempo trascorso quale strumento di riflessione critica; il diritto al

7 Black, op. cit., p. 6.

8 Ibid.

9 Sophia Kishkovsky, 'There is more to Malevich's Black Square than a hidden racist joke, Moscow curators reveal', *The Art Newspaper* (19 novembre 2015).

10 Black, op. cit., p. 8.

splitting in places like mudcrack, the traces of years of neglect sequestered in archives during the Soviet, particularly Stalinist, era, which preferred Socialist Realism over Malevich's (semantically worrying) Suprematist movement. The extralinguistic qualities of Gilroy's fractal allow for the revelations pertaining to *Black Square* to give birth to each other, making sense of, if nothing else, the bureaucracy of antiblackness. 'Expressed as fractals', Black concedes to a metaphor, 'freedom might be the freedom of freedom, freedom's freedom to free itself from freedom'.[11]

The first hundred or so words of Joy James and João Costa Vargas's co-written article 'Refusing Blackness-as-Victimization: Trayvon Martin and the Black Cyborgs' (2012) are similarly rhetorical, raising the question: what should – or will – happen when, 'instead of becoming enraged and shocked', we accept and recognise that the paradox of restorative 'justice' is that its prerequisite is '[producing or requiring] black exclusion and death as normative?'[12] To navigate this, James and Vargas propose the 'black cyborg' as capable of withstanding integration under the conditions of a capitalistic system structurally reliant on the invention and abstraction of the racialised subject, conjecturing a figure who is eligible for 'redemption from white racism' on account of their superhuman 'ethical, spiritual, and physical capabilities […] unusual strength, omniscience, and boundless love', characteristics that permit the black cyborg not only to exist but to thrive amid the paradoxical conditions of social reality and social death.[13] Implicitly castrated and existing on an interplanar level, the black cyborg – Afropessimist hero! – conveys, as James discusses years later, a necessary fearlessness to undertake the political project no one wants: having solidarity with 'disposable people' by '[going] to war with an empire'.[14] If rebellion is just part of devotion, and devotion is death driven, 'death can be your ability to be free…'.[15]

Following Achille Mbembe's conceptualisation of 'necropolitics', for which he inverts the Foucauldian concept of biopower, 'that domain of life over which power has taken control', to form *necropower*, the right to implement the power of death over life, citing the suicide bomber and the 'late-modern colonial occupation in Gaza and the West Bank' and Palestinian genocide as exemplary of this methodology, the 'necropolitical' has emerged in contemporary critical and artistic discourse as an actual and aesthetic category.[16] Both adjective and noun, it is not, however, infallible. Necropolitical methodology is sensitive to being undermined by the gratuity of its contents. Articulations on the Mediterranean as an aqueous, necropolitical intercontinental zone, for example, are faulted by over-compensatory forms, such as the map and its likeness: historically

11 Black, op. cit., 7.

12 João Costa Vargas and Joy A. James, 'Refusing Blackness-as-Victimization: Trayvon Martin: and the Black Cyborgs', in George Yancy and Janine Jones (eds.), *Pursuing Trayvon Martin Historical Contexts and Contemporary Manifestations of Racial Dynamics* (Lanham, MD: Lexington Books, 2012) 193.

13 Ibid., 198.

14 'Joy James: Fear Factor, Quantum Entanglement, and Revolutionary Love', op. cit.

15 Ibid.

16 Achille Mbembe, *Necropolitics* (Durham, NC: Duke University Press, 2019) 12.

decadimento concettuale e ontologico; il diritto della curiosità di uccidere i gatti; il diritto della storia di un'opera di andare in pezzi; e similmente il diritto di un'opera di smaterializzarsi. Una riproduzione digitale ridimensionata del quadrato, utilizzata per illustrare il testo di Black, ne rappresenta in modo chiaro lo stato di degrado: chiazze e spaccature in alcuni punti come fango secco, le tracce degli anni di incuria trascorsi negli archivi durante il sequestro dell'era sovietica, in particolare staliniana – era che preferiva il realismo socialista al movimento suprematista di Malevich (semanticamente preoccupante). Le qualità extralinguistiche del frattale di Gilroy permettono alle rivelazioni relative al *Quadrato Nero* di nascere l'una dall'altra, dando senso, se non altro, alla burocrazia dell'afrofobia. "Espressa come frattale", Black concede una metafora, "la libertà potrebbe essere la libertà della libertà, la libertà della libertà di liberarsi dalla libertà"[11].

Le prime centinaia di parole dell'articolo di Joy James e João Costa Vargas, "Refusing Blackness-as-Victimization: Trayvon Martin and the Black Cyborgs" (2012), sono retoriche in modo analogo e pongono la domanda: cosa dovrebbe accadere – o accadrà – quando, "anziché infuriarci e scandalizzarci", accetteremo e riconosceremo come normalità che il paradosso della "giustizia" riparativa è il prerequisito per "[produrre o richiedere] l'esclusione e la morte dei neri?"[12]. Per far questo, James e Vargas propongono il "cyborg nero" in quanto capace di resistere all'integrazione dettata dalle condizioni di un sistema capitalistico strutturalmente basato sull'invenzione e sull'astrazione del soggetto razzializzato, ipotizzando una figura idonea alla "redenzione dal razzismo bianco" in virtù delle sue sovrumane "capacità etiche, spirituali e fisiche [...] forza fuori dal comune, onniscienza e amore sconfinato", caratteristiche che permettono al cyborg nero non solo di esistere, ma anche di prosperare tra le condizioni paradossali della realtà sociale e della morte sociale[13]. Implicitamente castrato e presente a livello interplanare, il cyborg nero – eroe afropessimista! – trasmette, come James discuterà anni dopo, il coraggio necessario per intraprendere il progetto politico che nessuno vuole: essere solidali con "persone eliminabili", "[entrando] in guerra contro un impero"[14]. Se la ribellione è solo una parte del prendersi cura, e il prendersi cura è guidato dalla morte, "la morte può essere la tua possibilità di essere libero…"[15].

Attraverso la concettualizzazione di "necropolitica" avanzata da Achille Mbembe che sovverte il concetto foucaultiano di *biopotere* – ovvero "quell'ambito della vita su cui il potere ha preso il controllo" – viene teorizzato il *necropotere,* cioè il diritto di esercitare il potere della morte

11 Black, op. cit., p. 7.

12 João Costa Vargas, Joy A. James, 'Refusing Blackness-as-Victimization: Trayvon Martin: and the Black Cyborgs', *Pursuing Trayvon Martin Historical Contexts and Contemporary Manifestations of Racial Dynamics* (2012) p. 193.

13 Ibid., p. 198.

14 'Joy James: Fear Factor, Quantum Entanglement, and Revolutionary Love', op. cit.

15 Ibid.

an accelerant of early capitalistic behaviour and colonial speculation; contemporaneously, an open-source tool (such as Google Maps) appropriated and exploited by state forces to extend the panoptic and negatively securitised scope of European borderlands.[17] Moreover, the language sanctioned to publicly discuss the Mediterranean as a site of incidental death, let alone as necropolitical, is washed with pathetic fallacy, suggesting the naturality of shipwrecks in an objectively over-monitored zone.[18]

'The concrete emerges from the abstract, rather than the other way around,' Black advises. 'Mimesis is art at its most viciously abstract.'[19] The act of staging an already wrecked ship protects against the impasse of promulgating black death since the dead are already dead. Formalising assemblages of perishable, reactive materials as sculpture sets out the unstable precedent that a historical moment can be necessarily 'held', let alone preserved, by an institution, in turn drawing attention to the antithetical concept – to borrow from Saidiya Hartman – that 'the slave is the foundation of the national order' and at the same time 'occupies the position of the unthought', to which she asks: 'What does it mean to try to bring that position into view without making it a locus of positive value, or without trying to fill in the void?'[20]

Slippages (of language) happen all the time. When a sculpture is life-size but not life-like, for example, in spite of it indirectly relating to the presence of a body in terms of scale and finish, and implicating a subject where there is none, words tend to fail.

17 Laura Lo Presti, 'Like a Map Over Troubled Water: (Un)mapping the Mediterranean Sea's Terraqueous Necropolitics', *e-flux Journal*, no. 109 (May 2020) (e-flux.com/journal/109/330800/like-a-map-over-troubled-water-un-mapping-the-mediterranean-sea-s-terraqueous-necropolitics).

18 'Joy James: Fear Factor, Quantum Entanglement, and Revolutionary Love', op. cit.

19 Black, op. cit, 6.

20 Saidiya V. Hartman and Frank B. Wilderson III, 'The Position of the Unthought', *Qui Parle*, vol. 13, no. 2 (Spring–Summer 2003) 184–5.

sulla vita, citando il terrorista suicida, "l'occupazione coloniale tardo-moderna a Gaza e in Cisgiordania" e il genocidio palestinese come esemplificativi di questa metodologia, la "necropolitica" è emersa nel discorso critico e artistico contemporaneo come una categoria effettiva ed estetica[16]. Sia come aggettivo che come sostantivo, tuttavia, non è infallibile. La metodologia necropolitica tende ad essere minacciata dalla gratuità dei suoi argomenti. Gli sviluppi del Mediterraneo come zona intercontinentale acquatica e necropolitica, ad esempio, sono compromessi da forme iper-compensative, come la mappa e le sue derive: storicamente acceleratori dei primi comportamenti capitalistici e della speculazione coloniale; contemporaneamente, uno strumento open source, come Google Maps, sottratto e sfruttato dalle forze statali per estendere il raggio panottico e negativamente securizzato delle frontiere europee[17]. Inoltre, il linguaggio stabilito per discutere pubblicamente del Mediterraneo come sito di morte accidentale, per non dire addirittura necropolitico, è intriso di patetica fallacia, suggerendo la naturalità dei naufragi in una zona oggettivamente iper-monitorata[18].

"Il concreto emerge dall'astratto, piuttosto che il contrario" avverte Black. "La mimesi è l'arte al massimo della sua astrattezza"[19]. L'atto di esporre una nave già naufragata tutela dall'impasse di proclamare la morte nera, poiché i morti sono già morti. La produzione di assemblaggi di materiali deperibili e reattivi come sculture crea il precedente instabile secondo cui un momento storico può essere necessariamente "trattenuto", tantomeno conservato, da parte di un'istituzione; richiamando a sua volta l'attenzione sul concetto antitetico – per riprendere Saidiya Hartman – che "lo schiavo è il fondamento dell'ordine nazionale" e allo stesso tempo "occupa la posizione dell'ignorato", a cui l'artista chiede: "Che cosa significa cercare di portare alla luce questa posizione senza darne un'accezione positiva, o senza cercare di riempirne il vuoto?"[20].

Gli slittamenti (di linguaggio) avvengono di continuo. Quando una scultura è a grandezza naturale ma non è un oggetto reale, per esempio, malgrado si riferisca indirettamente alla presenza di un corpo in termini di dimensioni e qualità e implichi un soggetto che non c'è, le parole tendono a soccombere.

16 Achille Mbembe, *Necropolitics* (2019) p. 12.
17 Laura Lo Presti, 'Like a Map Over Troubled Water: (Un)mapping the Mediterranean Sea's Terraqueous Necropolitics', *e-flux Journal*, Issue #109 (maggio 2020) (e-flux.com/journal/109/330800/like-a-map-over-troubled-water-un-mapping-the-mediterranean-sea-s-terraqueous-necropolitics).
18 'Joy James: Fear Factor, Quantum Entanglement, and Revolutionary Love', op. cit.
19 Black, op. cit, p. 6.
20 Saidiya V. Hartman, Frank B. Wilderson III, 'The Position of the Unthought', *Qui Parle*, Vol. 13, No. 2 (primavera/estate 2003) pp. 184–5.

RACIAL PROFILE #3

A boat in the water
Not so big
Sails full
Or buckling
Or drenched
Or furled up tight and tied
To a torn-up masthead

A boat in the water
Not so big
A boat

Still in the water

PRESSURE AND SALT
FOR DOMINIQUE WHITE

ALEXIS PAULINE GUMBS

PRESSIONE E SALE
PER DOMINIQUE WHITE

This is for those of us who carry hurricane assignments. Our open hands. Our wild mouths. All of us children of pressure and salt who know that the wind connecting the west coast of africa, the caribbean volcanic arc and the east of the americas is a ceremony now. A dance of reckoning.

Many of us are in hiding. Whispering counterclockwise, whirling through quiet days. But not Dominique. Dominique leaves evidence. Daughter of salt and pressure, she suspends wreckage where you can see it, watch the contingency of net, rope, sail and metal fall apart.

You may think we are of one so-called race, the descendants, the targeted, the africans windswept into the americas in chains. You may think we are of one so-called species, human hands trying to undo what been done. You would be wrong.

Multitudes of us, in our uncountable cosmic Blackness, have a reason to study pressure. Salt.

Sharks listen for the storm. Through a series of fluid-filled canals, their whole body becomes an ear for balance. And when the barometric pressure shifts, like right before a hurricane, they know. And they decide. To leave for deeper water or to

Questo è per chi tra noi ha questo sentore per gli uragani. Le nostre mani aperte. Le nostre bocche selvagge. Tutti noi figli della pressione e del sale sappiamo che il vento che soffia dalla costa occidentale dell'africa all'arco vulcanico dei caraibi fino all'est delle americhe dà vita a una cerimonia. Una danza della resa dei conti.

Molti di noi si nascondono, sussurrando in senso antiorario, vorticando in giorni tranquilli. Ma non Dominique. Dominique lascia tracce. Figlia del sale e della pressione, tiene sospesi i relitti dove è possibile vederli, osservando la contingenza di reti, corde, vele e metalli sgretolarsi.

Potreste pensare che siamo di una stessa cosiddetta razza, i discendenti, i bersagli, gli africani sferzati dal vento in catene nelle americhe. Potreste pensare che siamo di una stessa cosiddetta specie, mani umane che cercano di disfare ciò che è stato fatto. Vi sbagliereste.

Molti di noi, nella nostra "Blackness" cosmica infinita, hanno un motivo per studiare la pressione. Il sale.

Lo squalo tende l'orecchio all'arrivo della tempesta. Attraverso una serie di canali colmi di fluidi, il suo corpo diventa un sensore per l'equilibrio. E quando la pressione barometrica cambia, come appena prima di un uragano, lo squalo lo sa. E deve decidere se andare verso acque più profonde oppure

stay and eat the mess. Usually the small sharks dive deep. Sometimes tiger sharks will stay and wait, trusting the risk of their own survival.

Dolphins taste the storm in stages. As the rain decreases the salt content in the water, they know the wind behind the rain is fierce. And they can't dive as deep as sharks, and so they salt-compass their bodies, move in the direction that promises more breath.

And you? How do you sense the suck of air, the unseasoned evidence at the edge of your next disaster?

Dominique has a practice that from some perspectives could look like salvage. But it's not. Since she knows that the colonising boat, the enslaving ship, the whale-hunting vessel is the model for the nation-states we now occupy or are displaced by, Dominique has chosen to make visible what she must have sensed, in the fluid under her skin. Must have tasted, in the food sweet captors offered. Must have heard and felt, in the listening she calls reading.

In one of the books she read, *In the Wake* by Christina Sharpe, Dominique held on to the idea of 'residence time'.

restare a mangiare ciò che rimane. Di solito uno squalo piccolo si immerge in profondità. Talvolta, invece, lo squalo tigre resta ad aspettare, confidando nelrischio della propria sopravvivenza.

Il delfino assaggia la tempesta gradualmente. Quando la pioggia diluisce il sale contenuto nell'acqua, lui riconosce la ferocia del vento. Il delfino non può immergersi in profondità come lo squalo, così rende il proprio corpo una bussola del sale per muoversi nella direzione che promette più respiro.

E voi? Come percepite il risucchio d'aria, il segnale che vi allerta all'orlo del vostro prossimo disastro?

Dominique ha una pratica artistica che da alcuni punti di vista potrebbe sembrare basata sul recupero degli oggetti. Ma non lo è, poiché sa che la nave colonizzatrice, negriera e cacciatrice di balene è il modello degli Stati-nazione che ora occupiamo o da cui siamo sfollati. Dominique ha scelto di rendere visibile ciò che deve aver percepito nel fluido sottopelle; ciò che deve aver assaggiato nel cibo offerto dai suoi amorevoli rapitori; ciò che deve aver sentito e provato in quell'ascolto che lei chiama lettura.

In uno dei libri che ha letto, *In the Wake* di Christina Sharpe, Dominique ha acquisito la nozione del "tempo di permanenza": il tempo di permanenza del suono nell'oceano.

The length of time sound lingers in the ocean.

In one of the books she may have read, *Specters of the Atlantic* by Ian Baucom, Dominique would have noticed fungibility. The insurance language for bodies torn apart.

In one of the books she read, *Undrowned* by Alexis Pauline Gumbs, she marvelled at the fugitivity of marine mammals. The most successful fugitives being the ones scientists cannot track.

From these and other sources. The water vapour of her conversations. From these and other sources. The salt of her own tears. From these and other sources. The dissonance in her own education. She crafted her uncraft. The opposite of shipping. She uncrafted a black practice in public. Falling apart.

Or maybe I'm projecting.

The western domination of the world was made by ships. The idea of a bounded, airtight social order. The risk of edges. The idea of scarce supply fashions life on land on every continent now. We have internalised it. Our colonial training is to act like land mammals stranded at sea. Even when we're off the boat.

In uno dei libri che potrebbe aver letto, *Specters of the Atlantic* di Ian Baucom, Dominique avrebbe potuto notare l'idea di fungibilità: il linguaggio previdenziale per i corpi fatti a pezzi.

In uno dei libri che ha letto, *Undrowned* di Alexis Pauline Gumbs, si è meravigliata della fuggevolezza dei mammiferi marini; essendo i fuggitivi più abili quelli che gli scienziati non riescono a rintracciare. Da queste e altre fonti: il vapore acqueo delle sue conversazioni. Da queste e altre fonti: il sale delle sue stesse lacrime. Da queste e altre fonti: la dissonanza della sua educazione. Ha formato ciò che non aveva forma. Il contrario del navigare. Ha decostruito in pubblico una pratica nera. Cadendo a pezzi.

O forse sto proiettando.

Il dominio occidentale del mondo è stato compiuto dalle navi. L'idea di un ordine sociale ermetico e delimitato. Il rischio dei margini. L'idea della scarsità delle risorse caratterizza ora la vita sulla terraferma in tutti i continenti. L'abbiamo interiorizzata. Il nostro addestramento coloniale ci impone di comportarci come mammiferi terrestri incagliati in mare, perfino quando siamo fuori dalla barca.

Anche la percezione di me è nautica. Principalmente il fatto di navigare nella conoscenza, anche quando questa prende altri nomi. Così come imbarcarsi nelle relazioni.

My sense of myself is also made of ships. Mostly scholar-ships, even when under other names. Also relationships. The ways I stay afloat.

Dominique's installations. Suspended and pulling themselves down. Placed and unravelling. Remind me of the invisible ocean shaping our life on earth. That if I was ever a land mammal it's too late now. I'm swimming in context.

Sharks sense pressure. Dolphins taste salt. What if it was not the trail of murders, bodies thrown overboard that caused sharks and dolphins to flank enslaving ships on their hurricane route journey across the atlantic? What if it was another sense?

Kinship? Witness?

Even if it was the fecundity of the blood of my ancestors they were after, what can that possibly mean? The salt. The helix. The bacterial persistence. What guidance, what symbiosis lives in the material fact that sharks, dolphins and grey whales and other marine mammals physically processed that particular salt, the embodied codes of kidnapped ancestral flesh, into an ocean ecosystem.

I modi in cui rimango a galla.

Le installazioni di Dominique. Sospese, si trascinano giù. Posizionate, si svelano. Mi ricordano l'oceano invisibile che dà forma alla nostra vita sulla terra. Se anche fossi mai stata un mammifero terrestre, ormai è troppo tardi. Sto nuotando nel contesto.

Gli squali percepiscono la pressione. I delfini distinguono il sapore del sale. E se non fosse stata la scia di omicidi, di corpi gettati in mare a far sì che squali e delfini affiancassero le navi negriere nel loro viaggio attraverso l'atlantico sulla rotta degli uragani? E se fosse stato qualcos'altro?

Essere parenti? Essere testimoni?

Anche se fosse stata la fecondità del sangue dei miei ante-nati ciò che cercavano, cosa potrebbe voler dire? Il sale. L'elica. La persistenza batterica. Quale orientamento, quale simbiosi risiede nella contingenza per cui squali, delfini, balene grigie e altri mammiferi marini hanno fisicamente trasformato quel particolare sale - ovvero i codici impersonificati dalla carne rapita degli antenati - in un ecosistema oceanico.

Credo che, alla fine, sul disastro del capitalismo, della schiavitù e del colonialismo, vorrei dire che, contrariamente alle logiche che hanno alimentato quel disastro (grazie Sylvia Wynter), nessuna traiettoria è meramente lineare e, inoltre, più di una cosa sempre accade, anche se si finge che il tempo è unitario. Penso a M. Jacqui Alexander, che in *Pedagogies of*

I guess what I finally need to say about the disaster of capitalism, slavery and colonialism is that, counter to the logics that fuelled that disaster (thank you, Sylvia Wynter), no trajectory is merely linear and more than one thing is always happening, even if you pretend time is unitary. I think about M. Jacqui Alexander, who taught us in *Pedagogies of Crossing* that the middle passage was, in addition to everything else that it was, an energy transfer of the elemental deities of the african continent, across the planet because all water is connected to all water everywhere.

I believe her. And every lifeform, bacterial to mammoth, participated in that movement of energy. Yes the whales, yes the sharks, yes the dolphins, algae too. With their very bodies.

And in this body. Which is mostly a transportation vector for bacteria, I am processing energy too. I am learning from shark relatives to notice the pressure warnings and guidance right beneath my skin. I am learning from dolphin relatives to notice the balance, imbalance of salt. Now move. Now stay. I become barometric in my being, *because you ain't heard? Oh no. Hurricane ain't done.*

Crossing ci ha insegnato che il *middle passage* [passaggio di mezzo] era, oltre a tutto il resto, un trasferimento energetico delle divinità elementali del continente africano, attraverso il pianeta, dal momento che tutta l'acqua è connessa a tutto il resto dell'acqua, ovunque.

Le credo. E ogni forma di vita, dal batterio al mammut, ha partecipato a questo movimento di energia. Così le balene, così gli squali, così i delfini, persino le alghe. Proprio con i loro corpi.

E in questo corpo, che è soprattutto un vettore per il trasporto dei batteri, anch'io sto elaborando energia. Sto imparando dagli squali, miei parenti, a percepire l'avvertimento della pressione e la sua guida proprio sotto la mia pelle. Sto imparando dai delfini, miei parenti, a capire l'equilibrio e il disequilibrio del sale. Ora muovendomi, ora stando ferma. Sto diventando barometrica nel mio essere, *perché, non l'hai sentito? Oh no. L'uragano, non ha ancora finito.*

Or
suppose that gorgeous
wings spread
speckled
hawk
begins to glide
above my body lying
down
like dead meat
maybe start to rot
a little bit
not moving
see just flat
just limp
but hot
not moving
see
him circle closer
closing closer
for the kill
until
he makes that dive
to savage
me
and inches
from the blood flood lusty
beak
I roll away
I speak
I laugh out loud
Not yet
big bird of prey
not yet

JUNE JORDAN

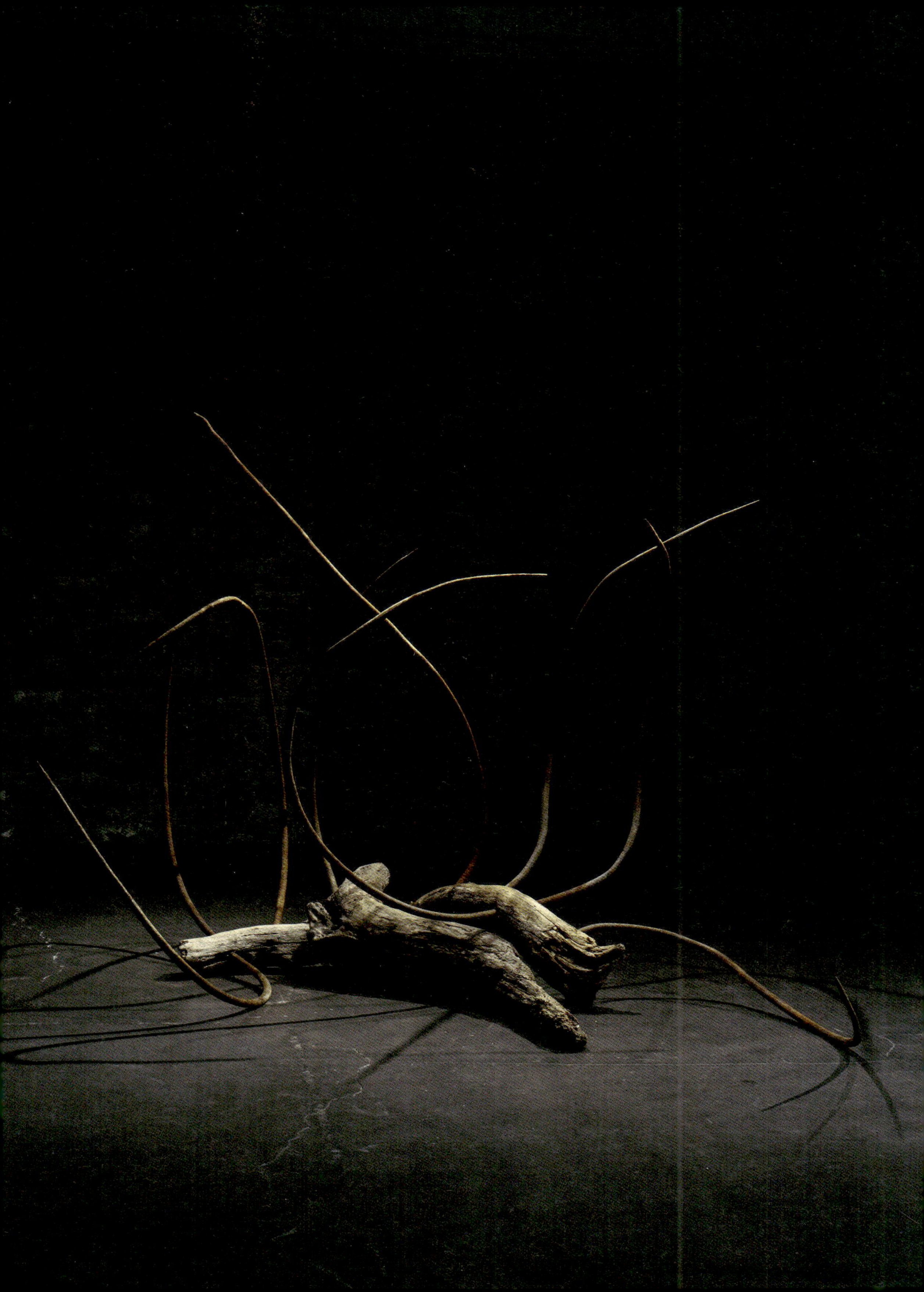

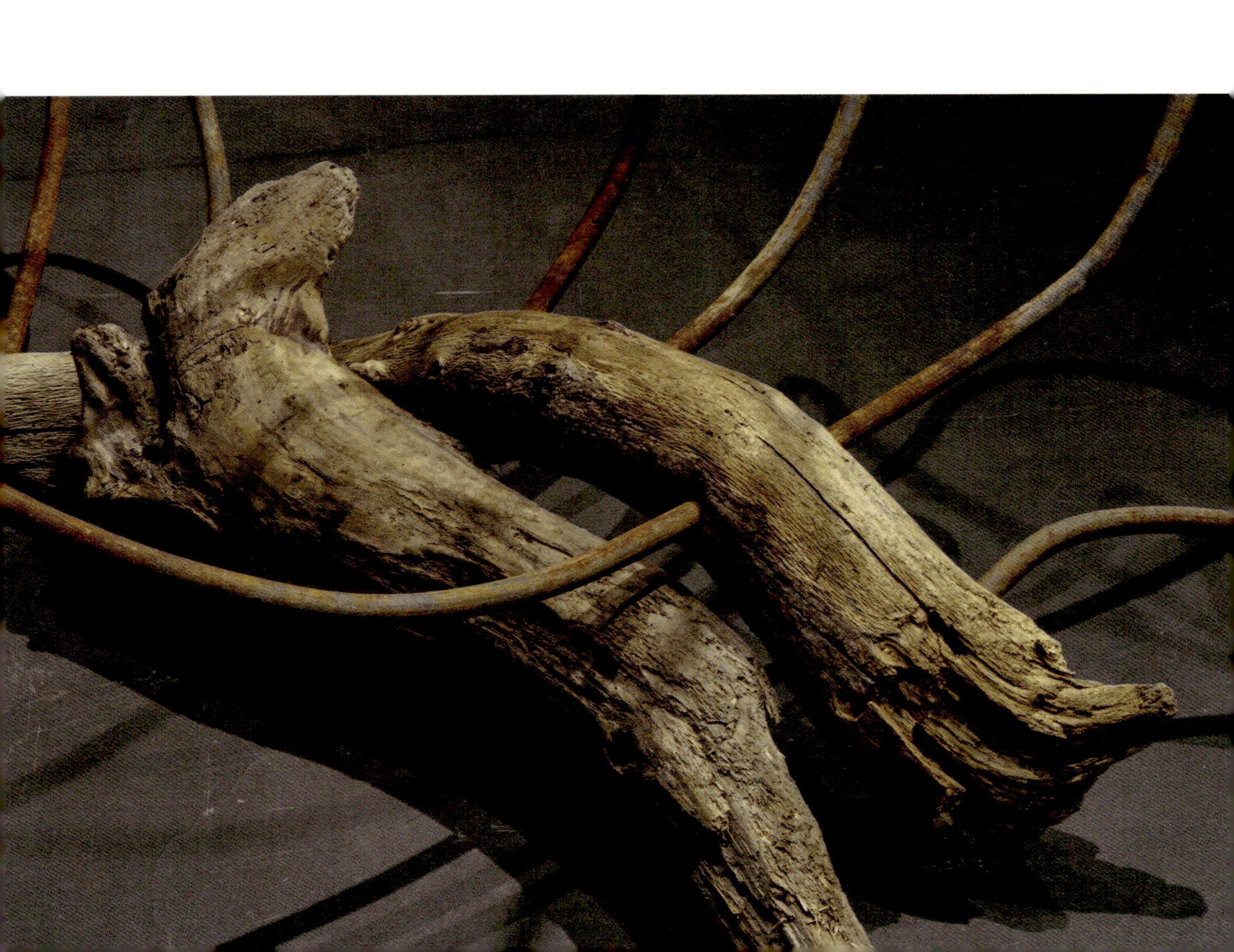

INELIGIBLE FOR DEATH (2024) Driftwood, forged iron / Legname, ferro forgiato

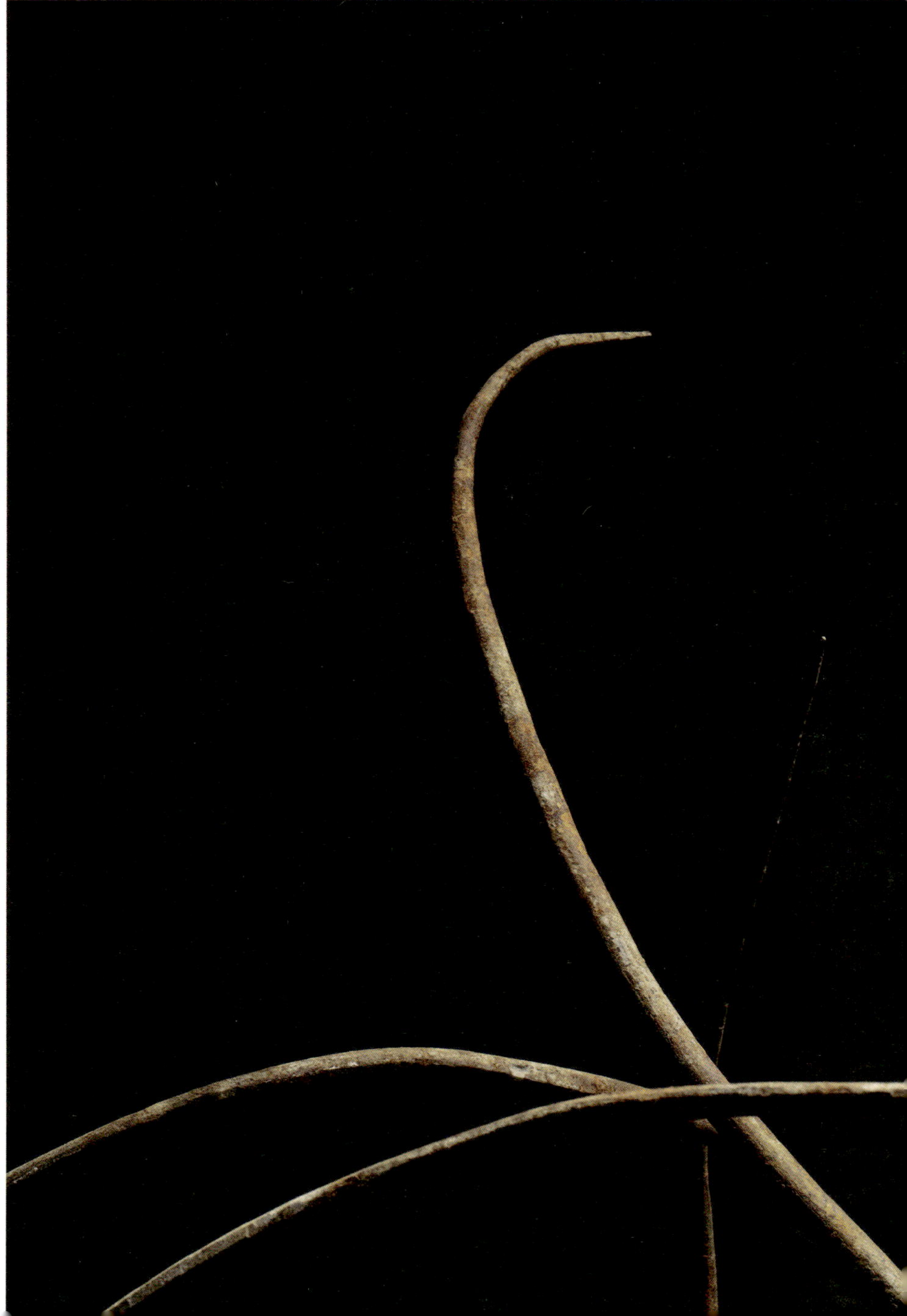

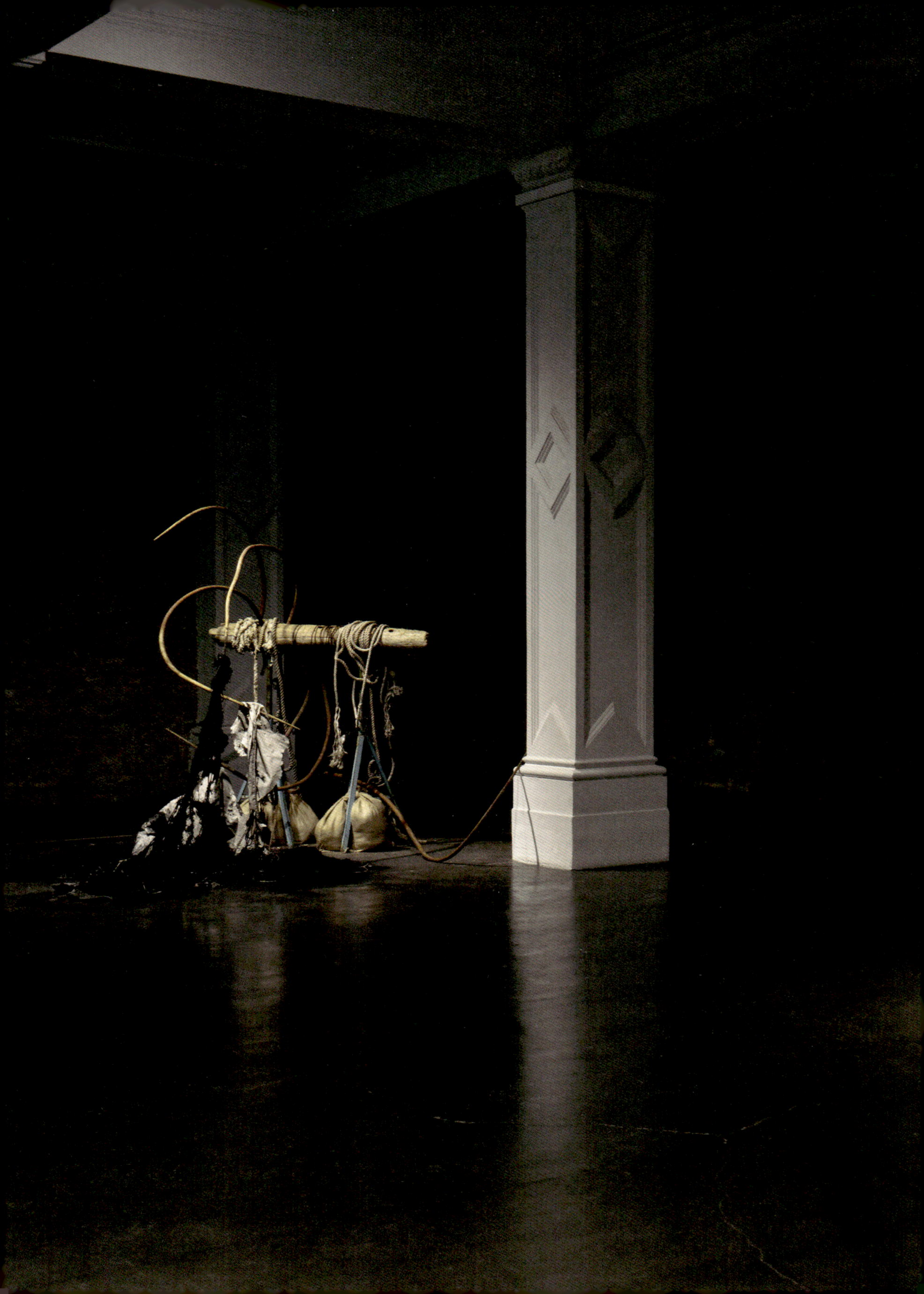

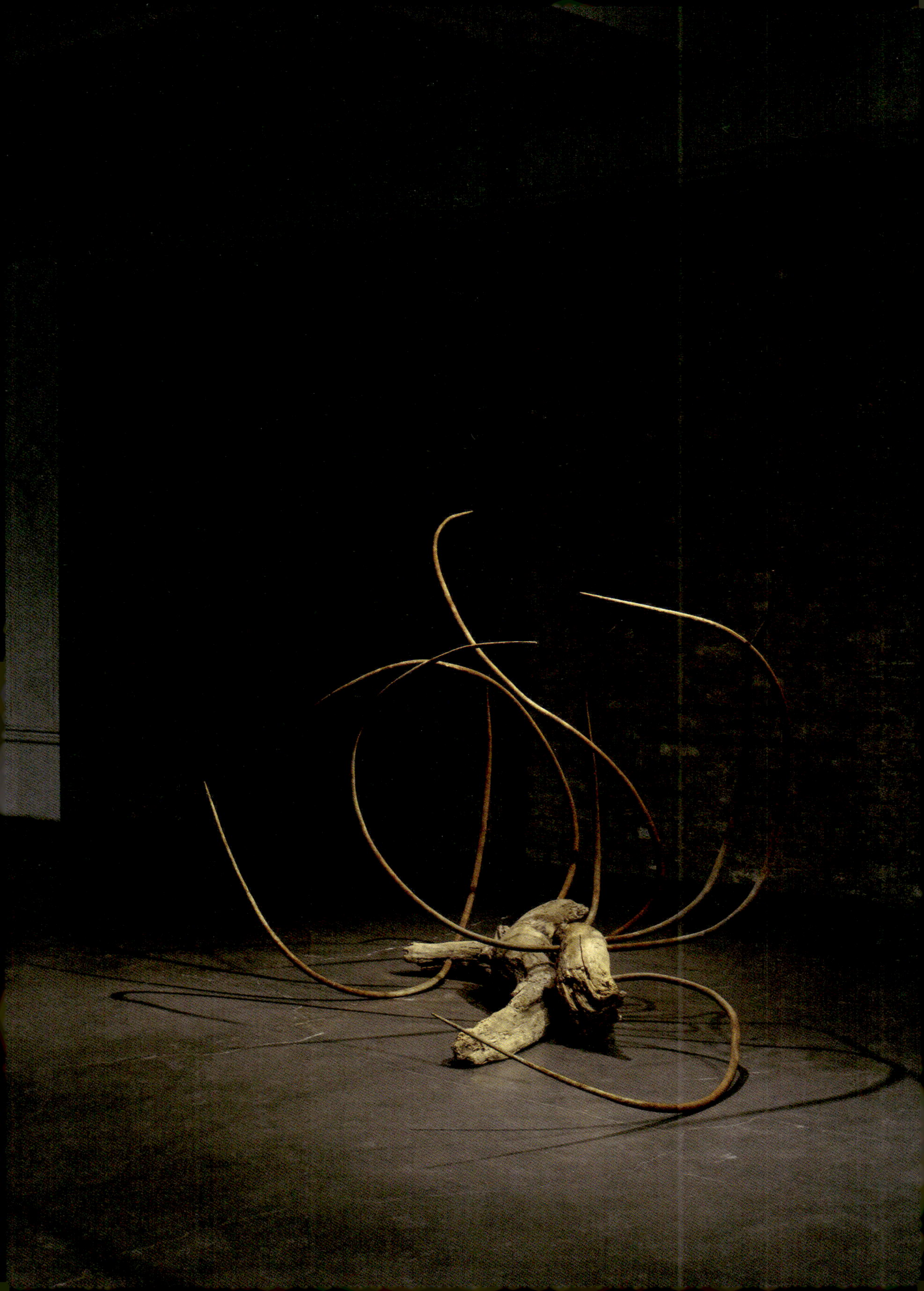

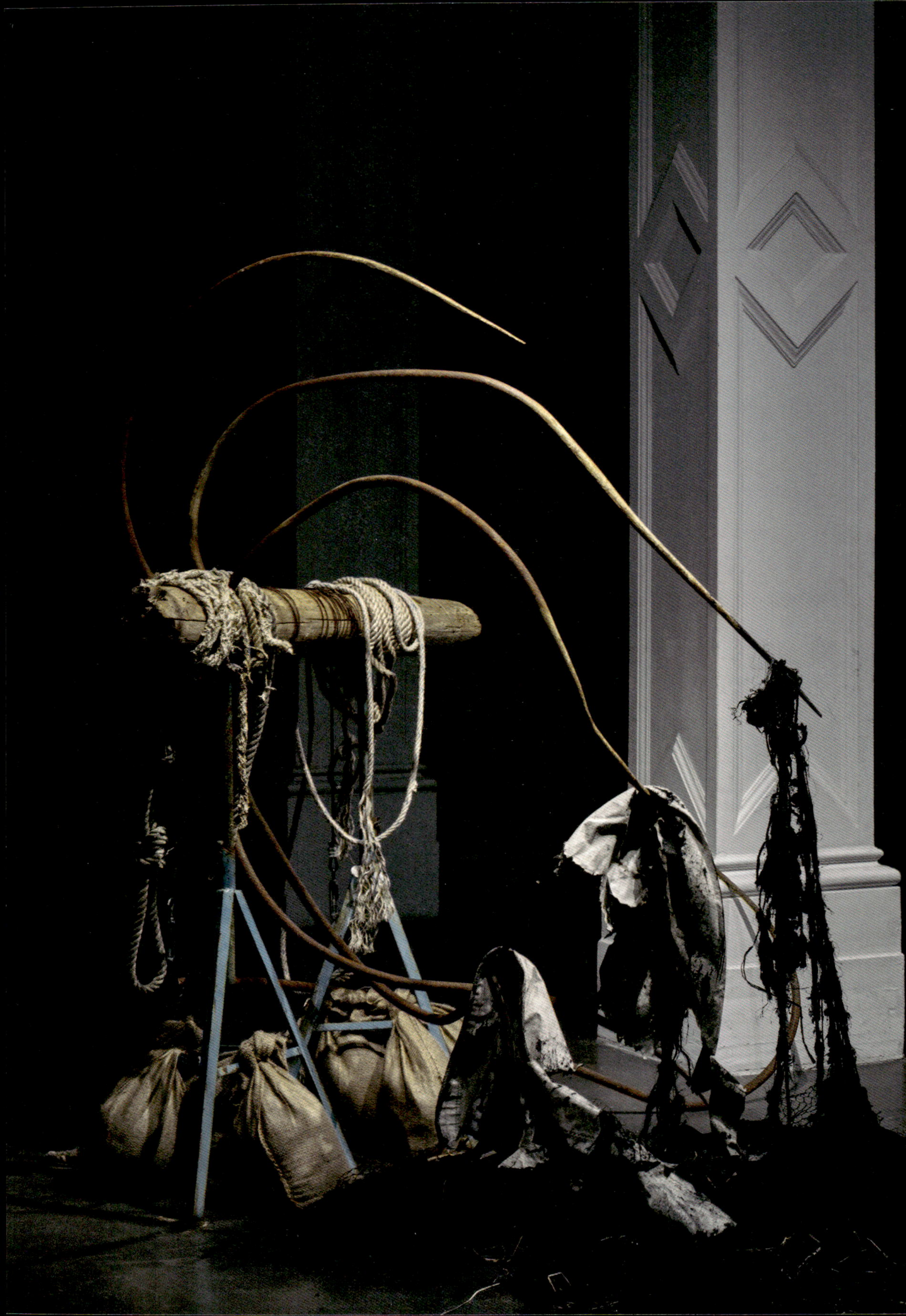

SPLIT OBLITERATION (2024) Driftwood, high volatile charcoal, forged iron, metal wire, sisal, raffia, destroyed sails, exhausted ropes / Legname, carbone polverizzato, ferro forgiato, fil di ferro, sisal, rafia, vele danneggiate, cordoni consumati

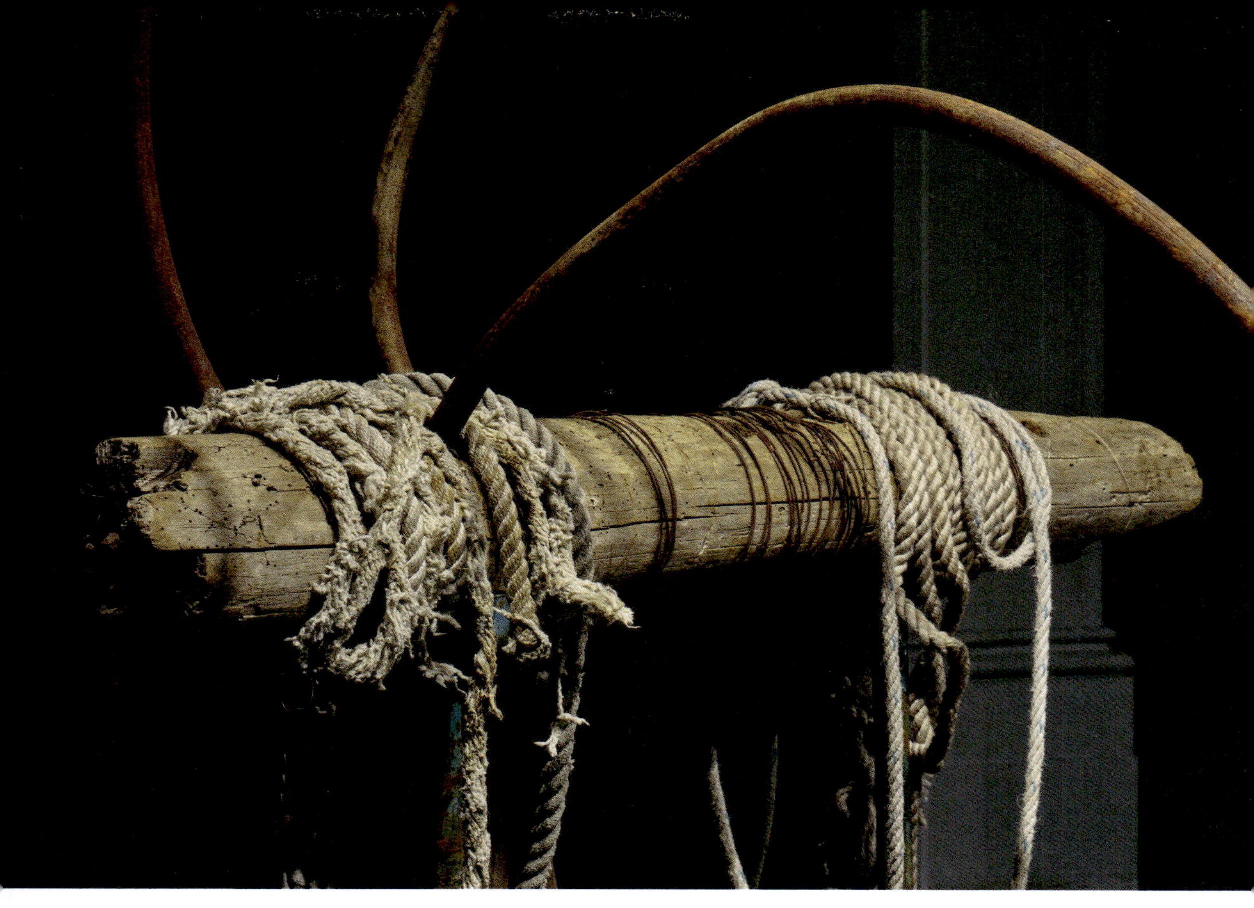

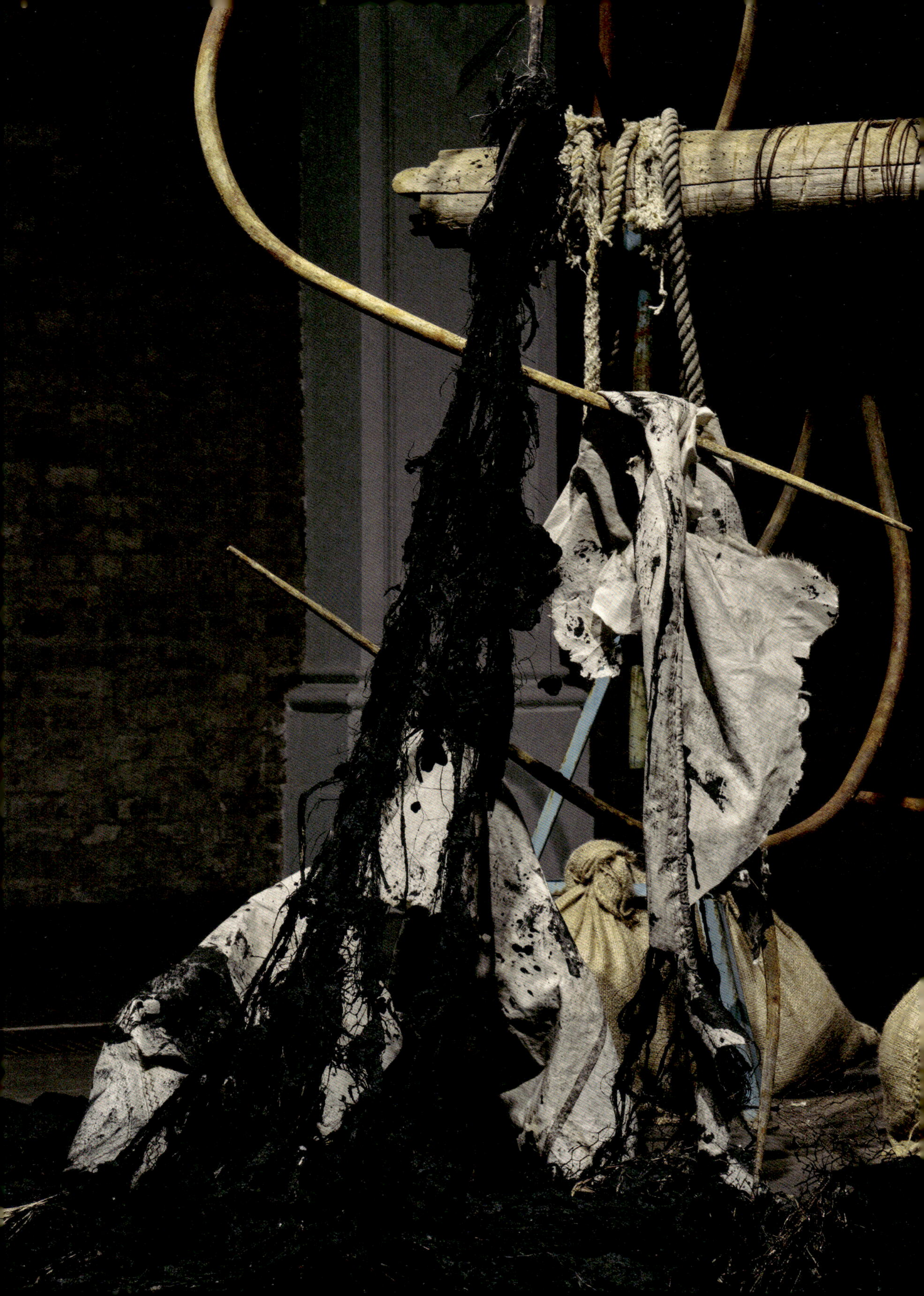

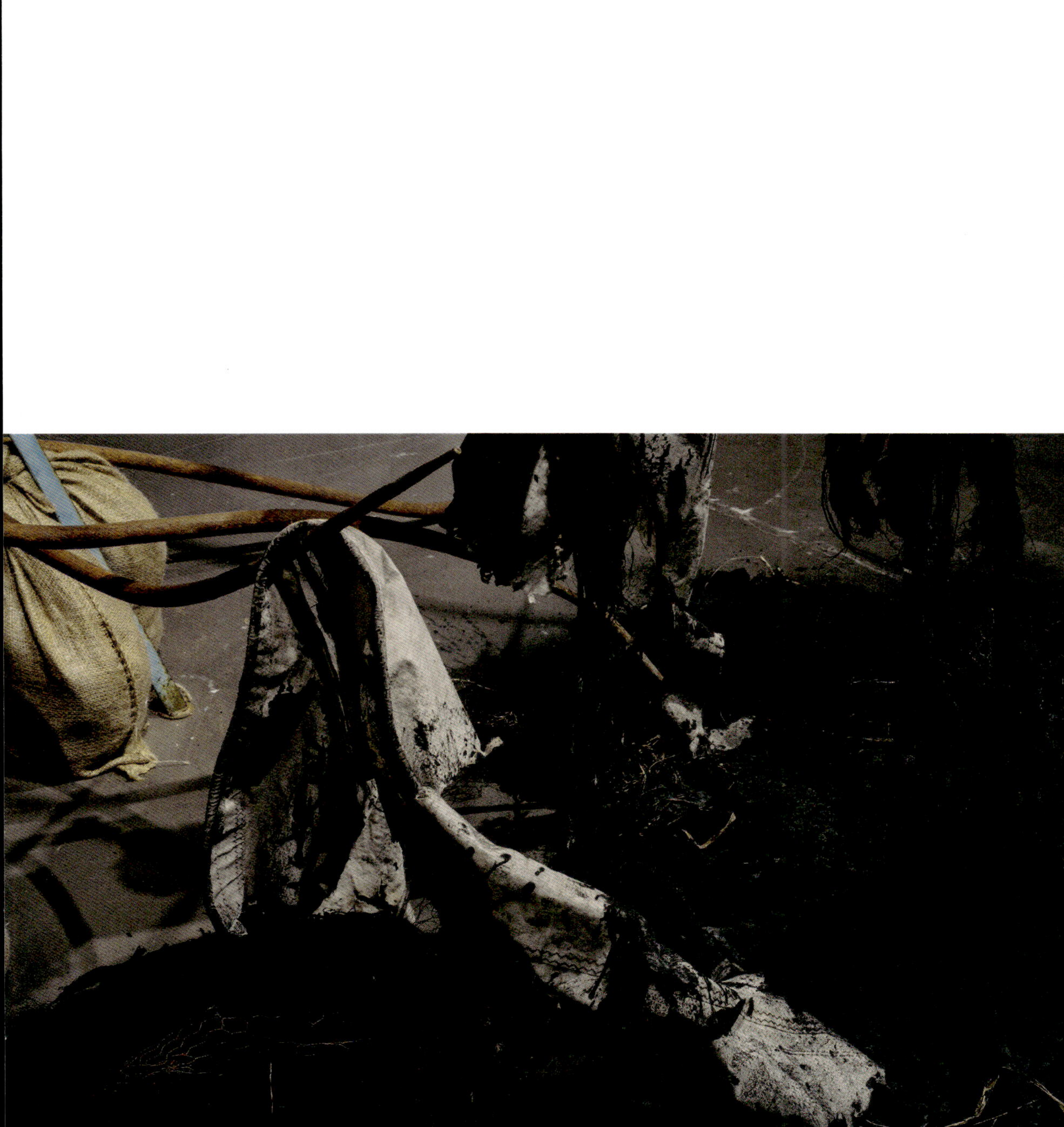

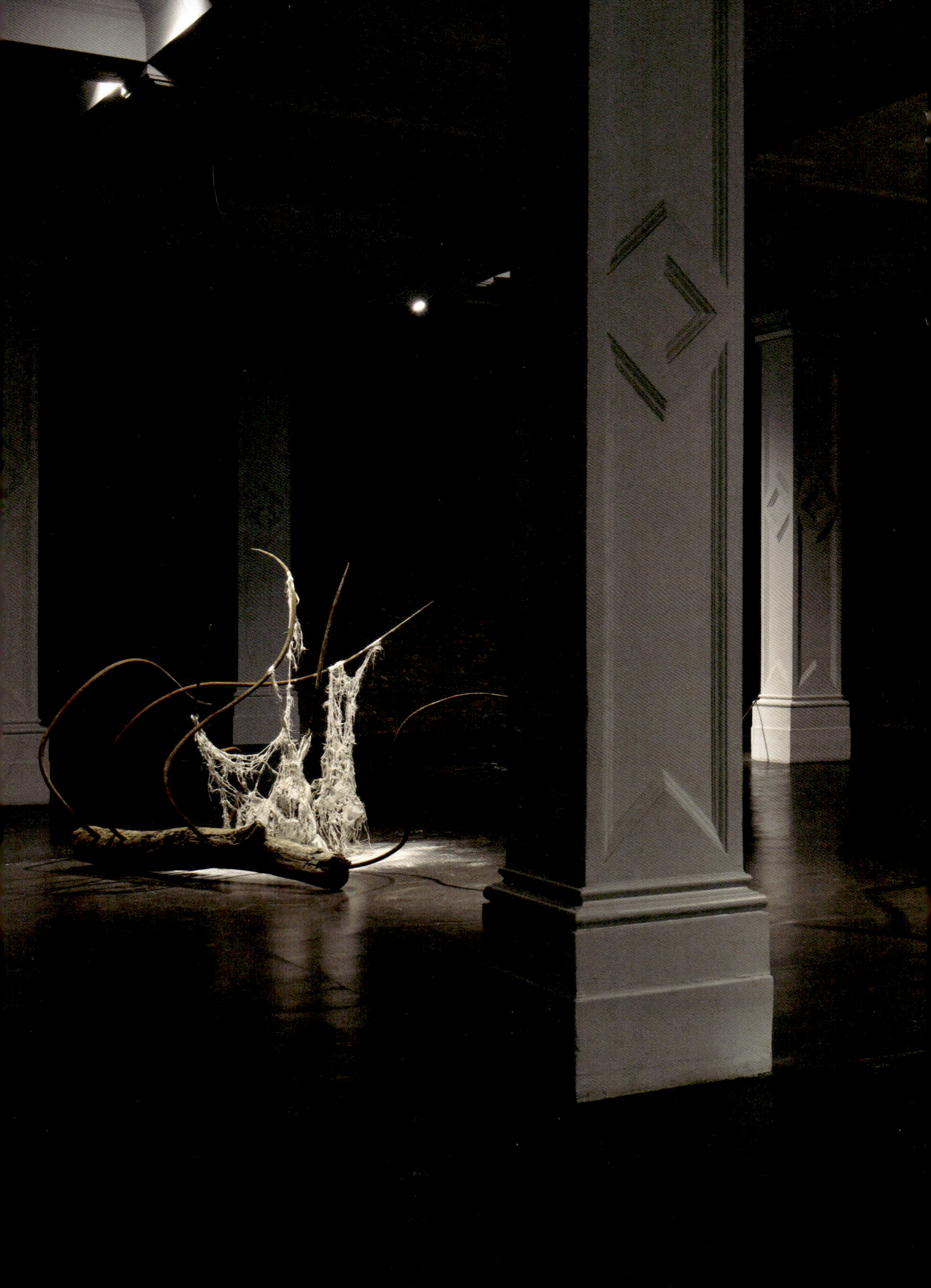

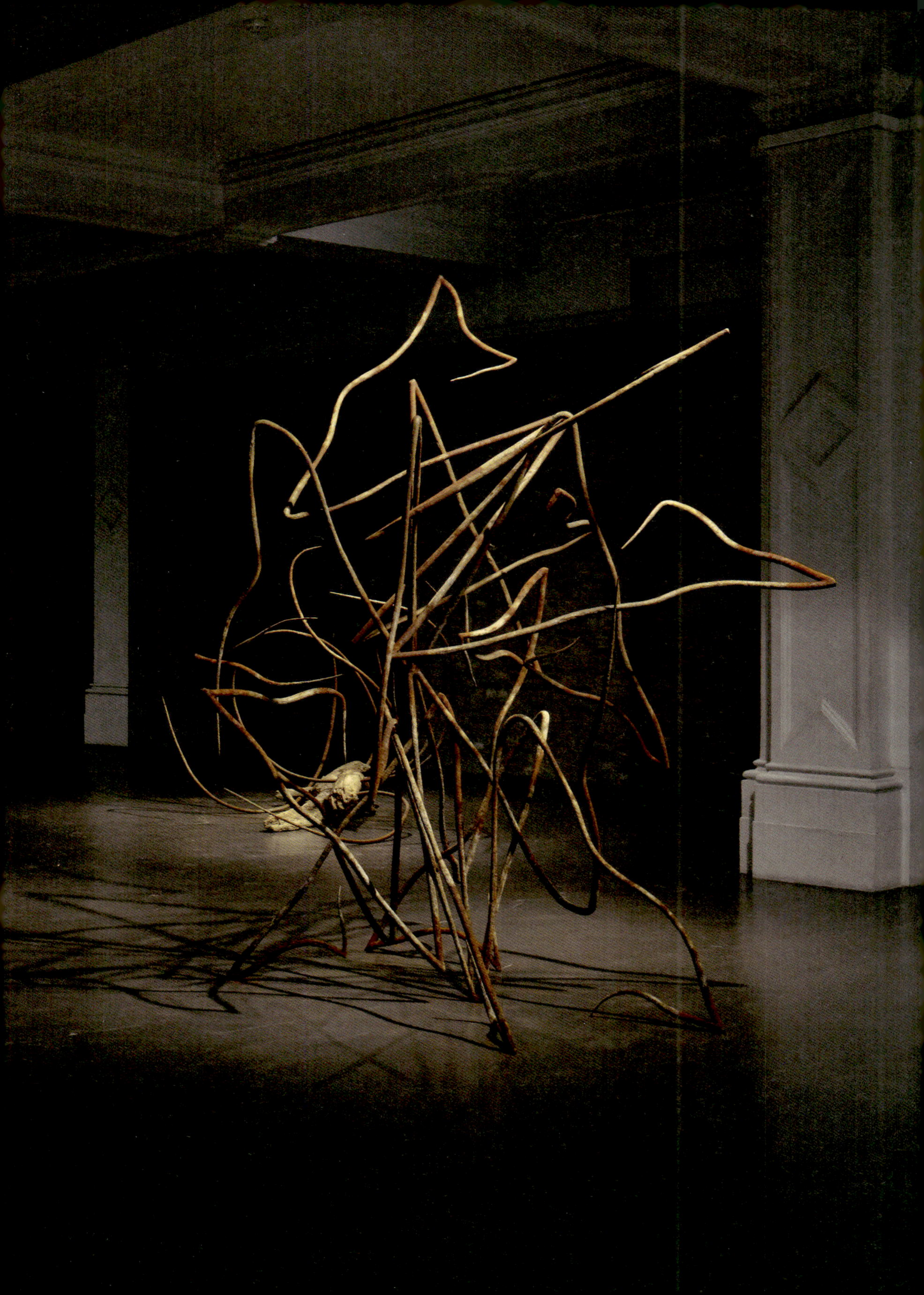

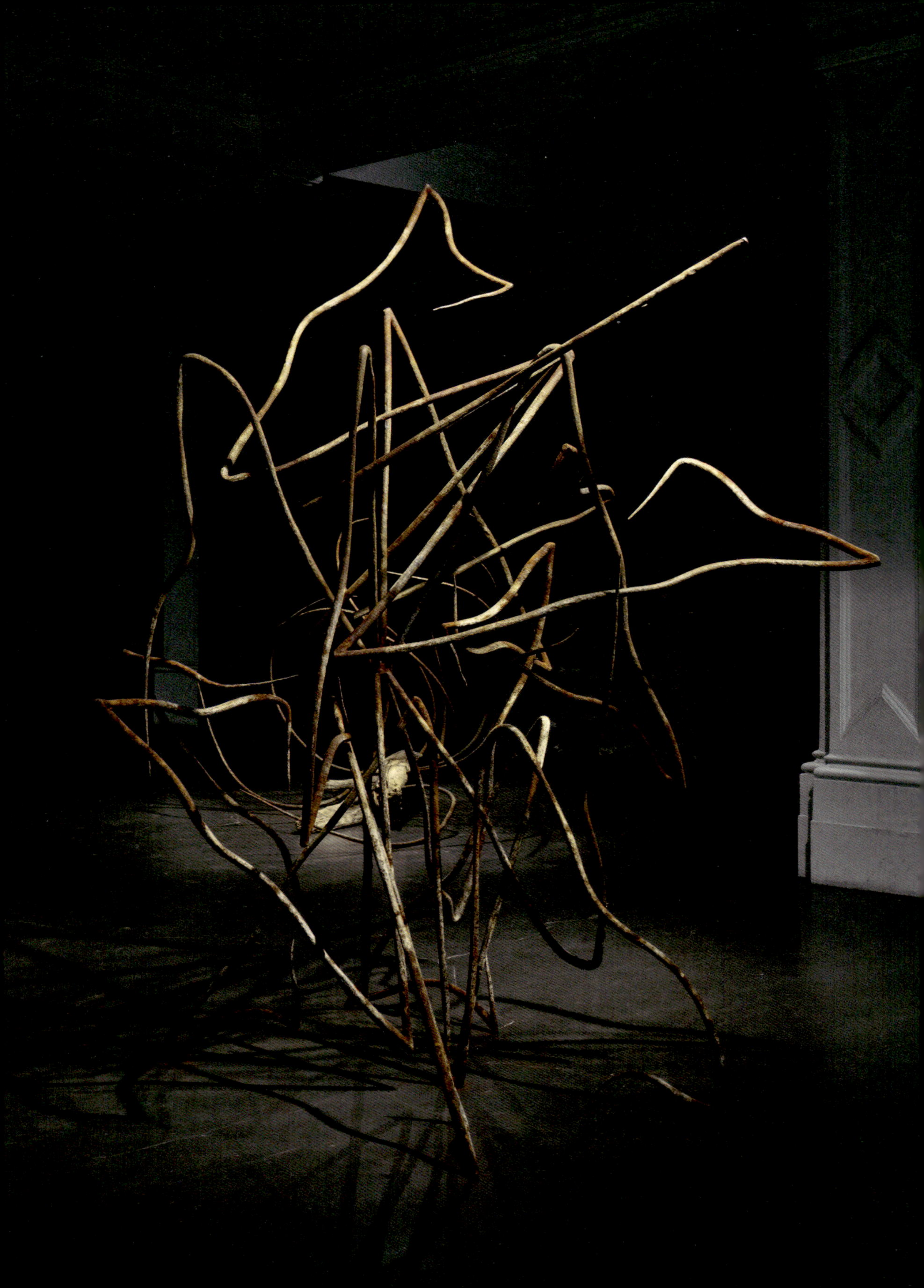

DEAD RECKONING (2024) Forged iron / Ferro forgiato

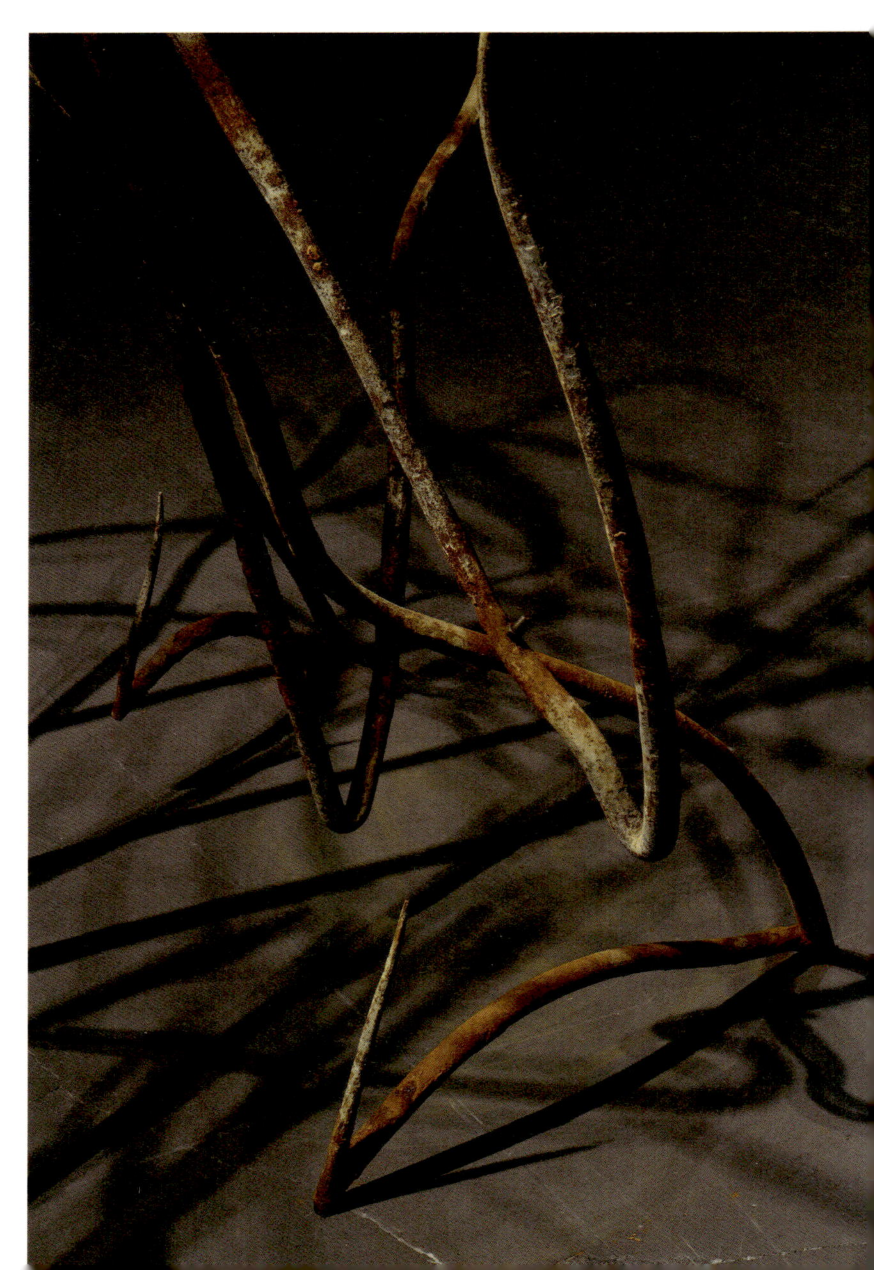

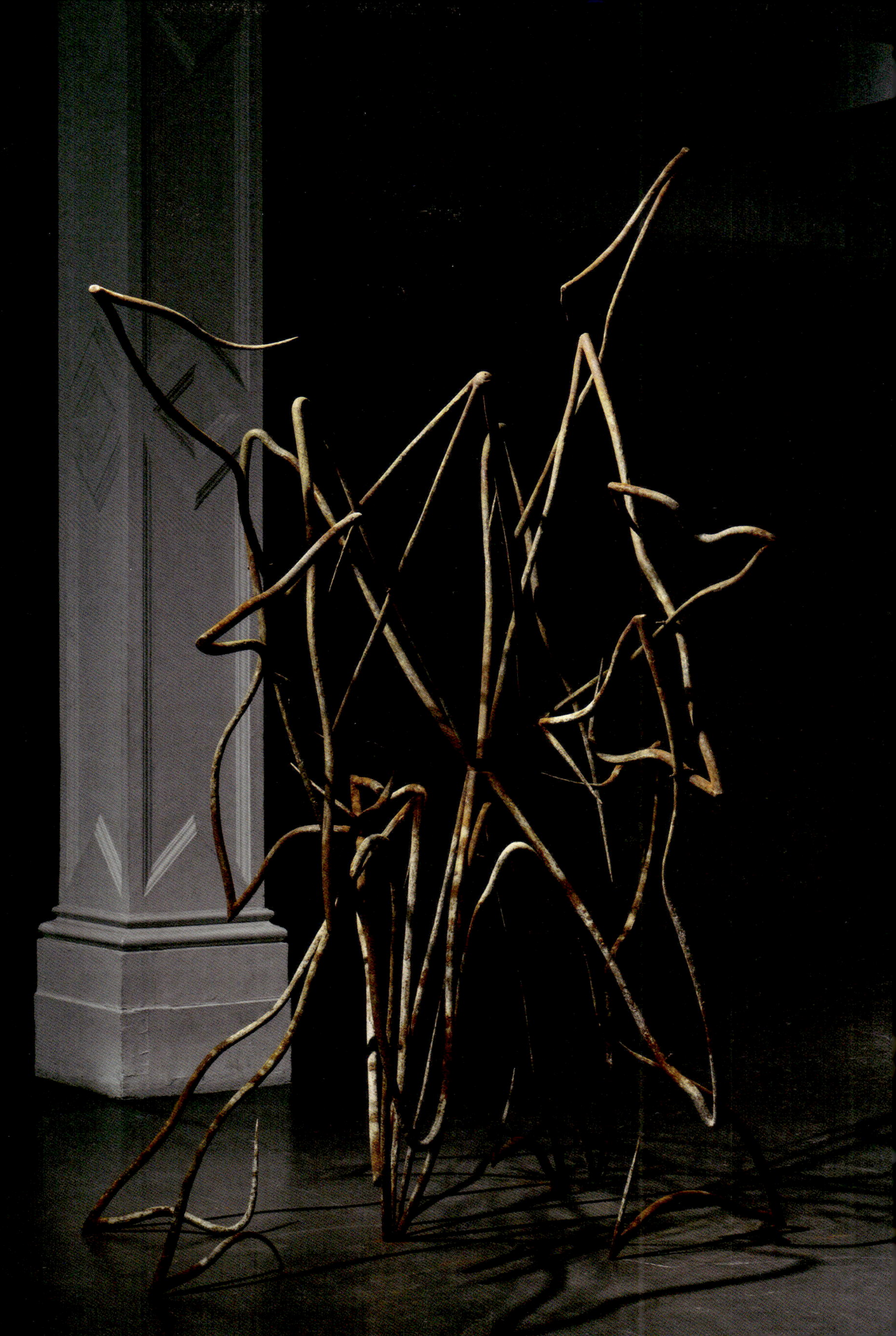

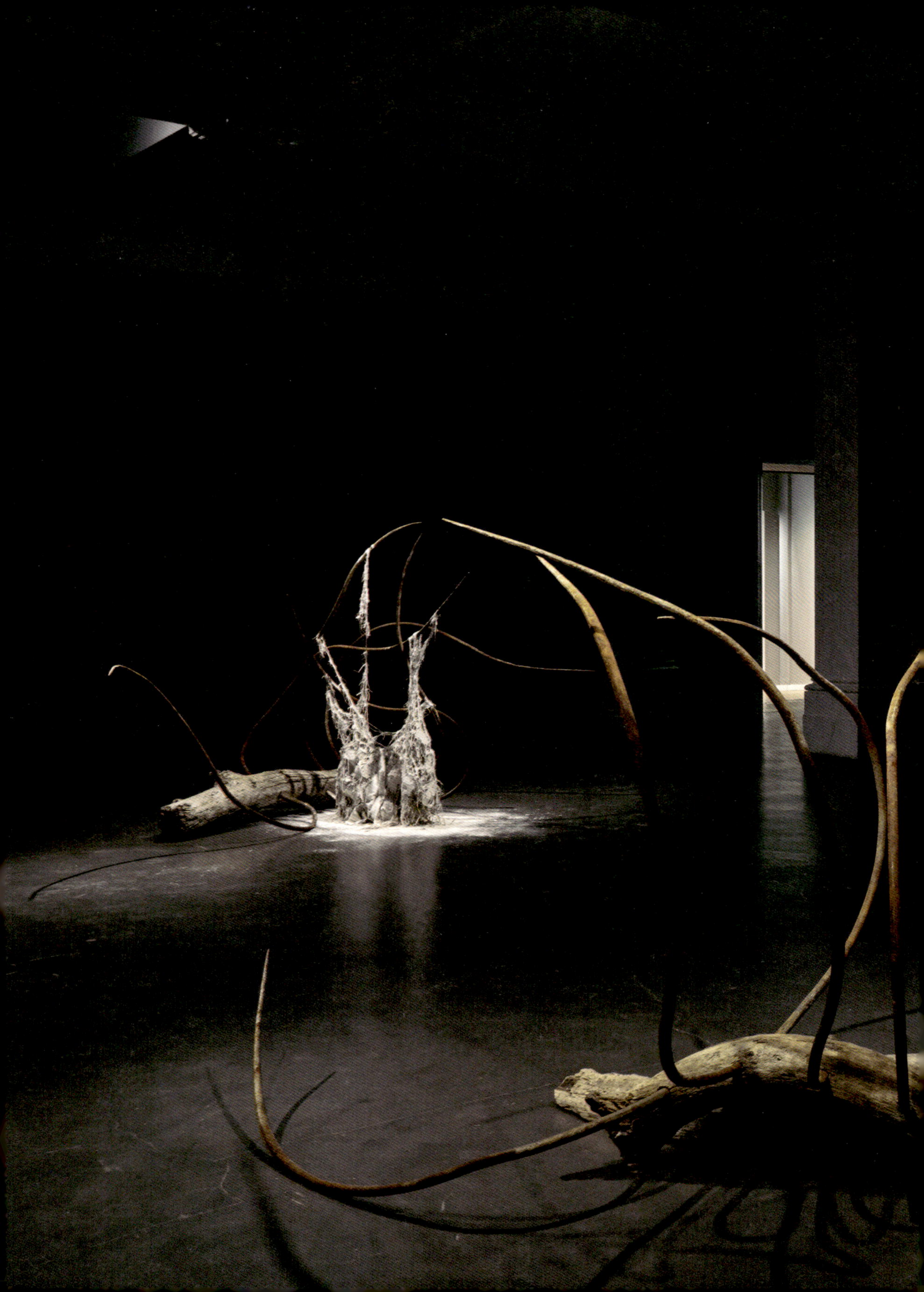

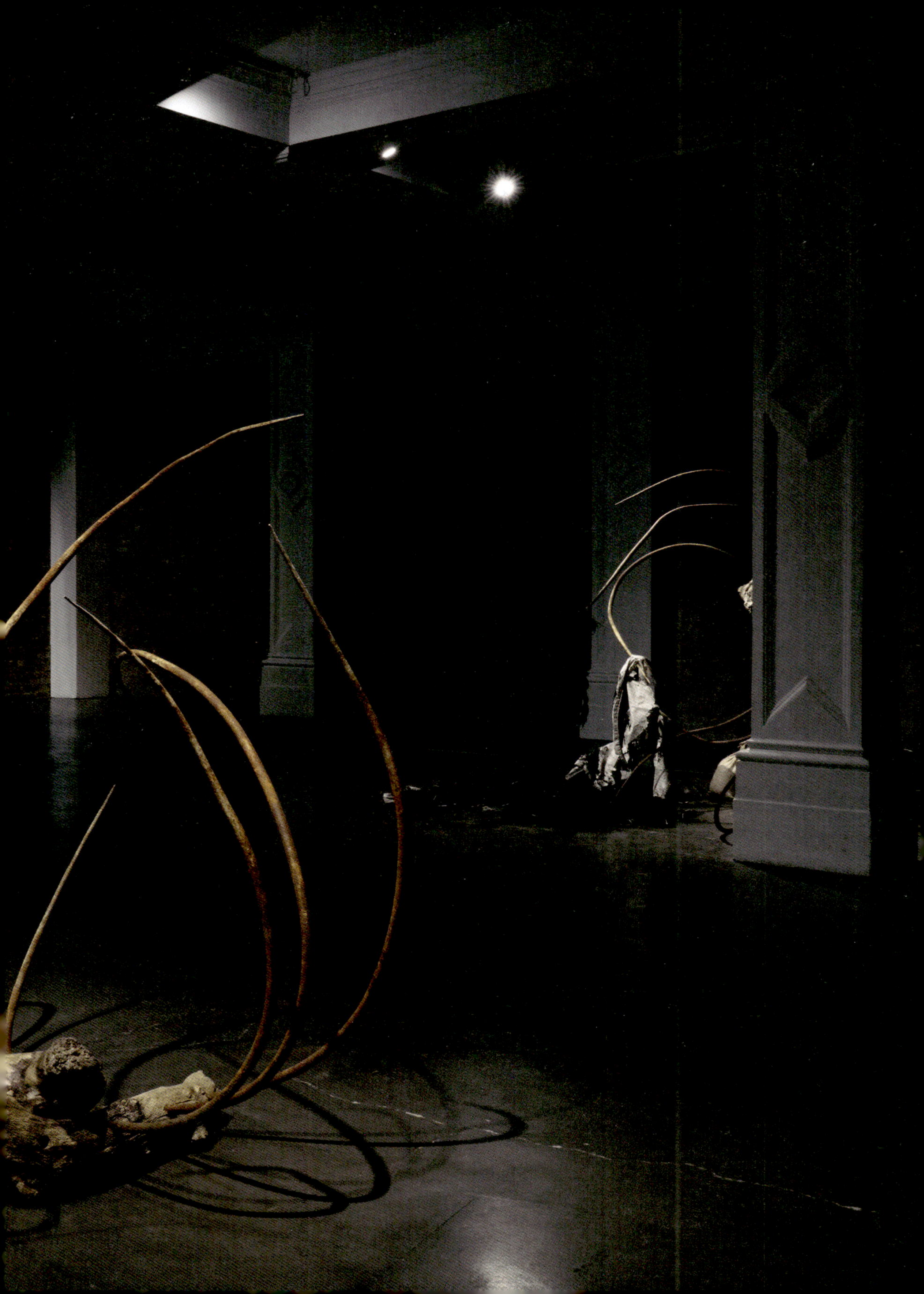

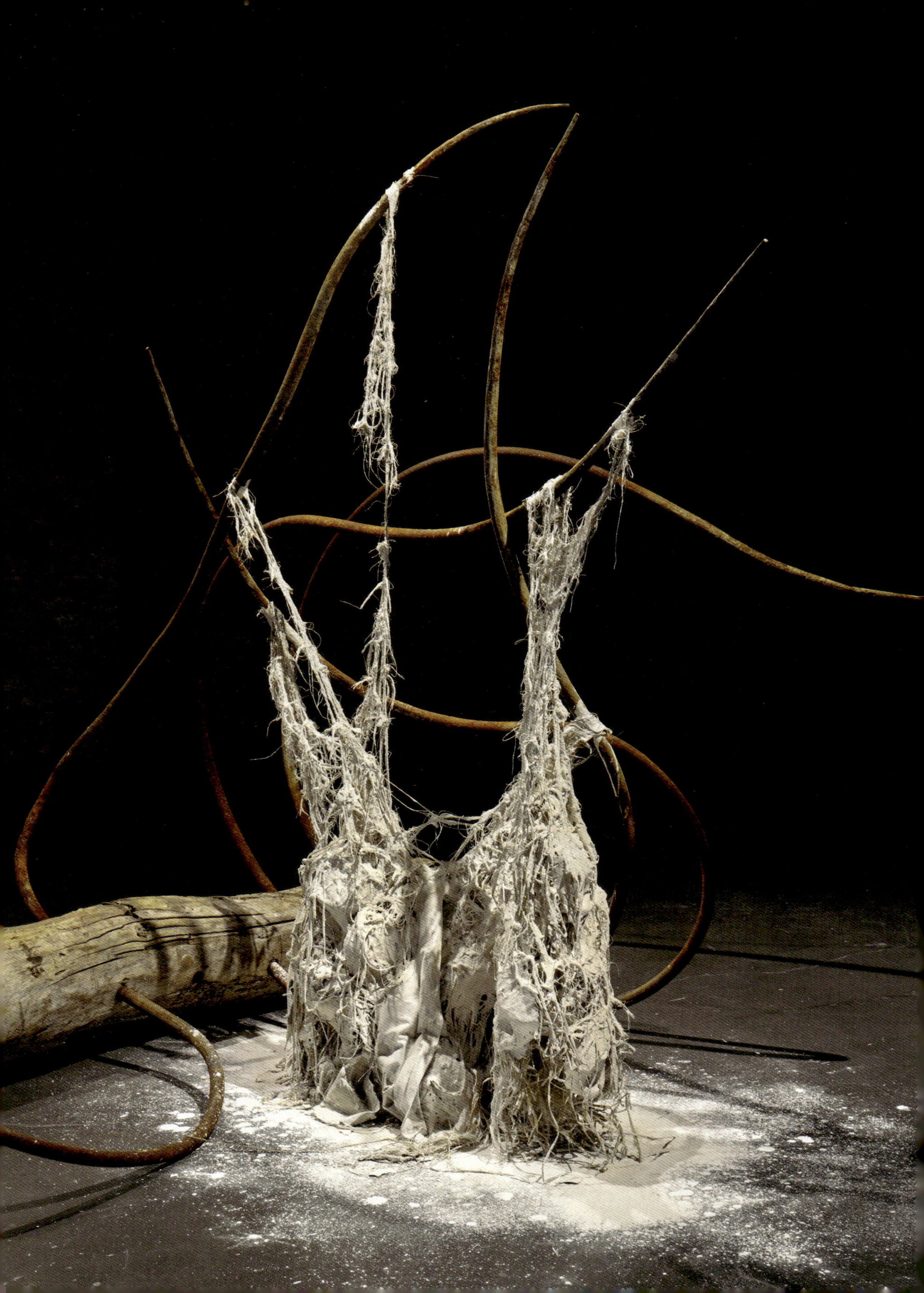

THE SWELLING ENEMY (2024) Driftwood, forged iron, sisal, raffia, kaolin clay, destroyed sails / Legname, ferro forgiato, sisal, rafia, argilla caolino, vele danneggiate

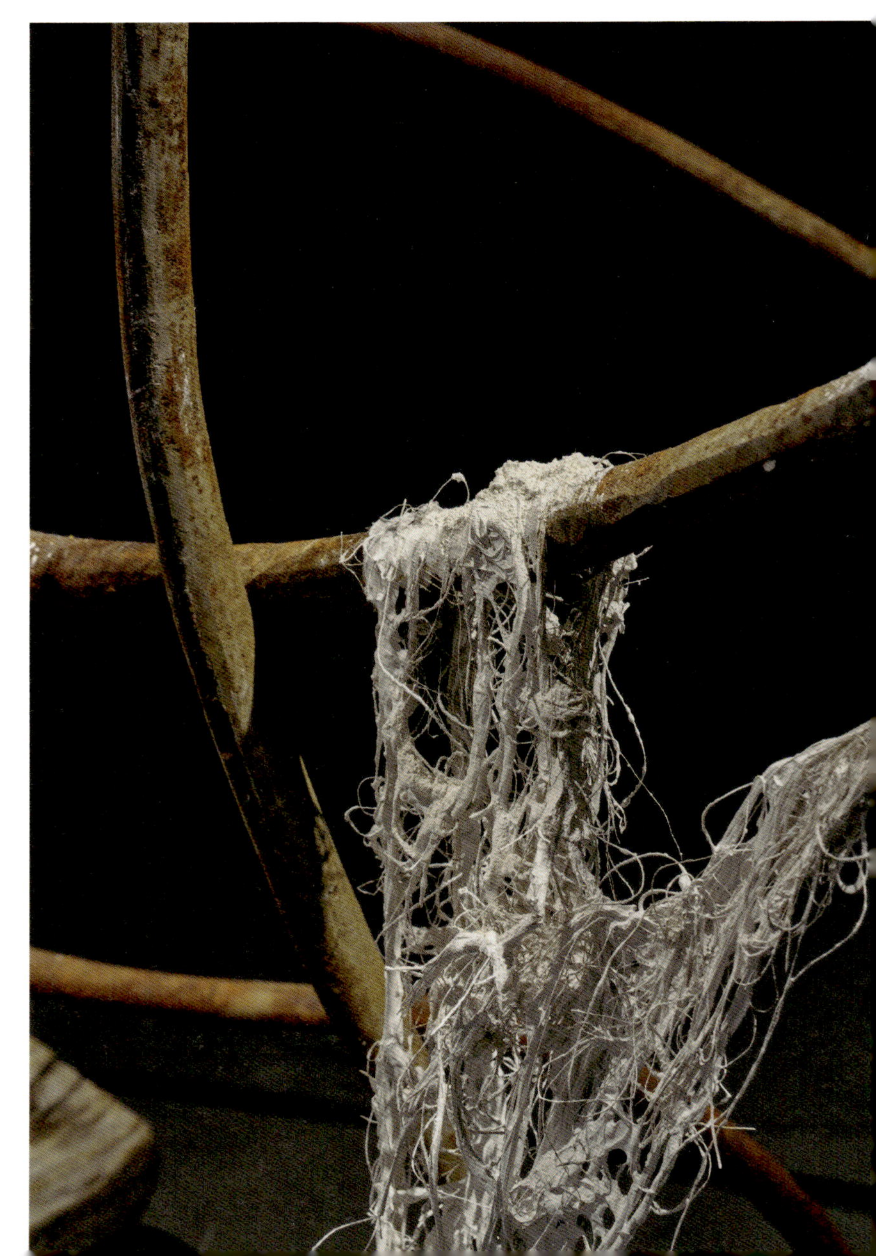

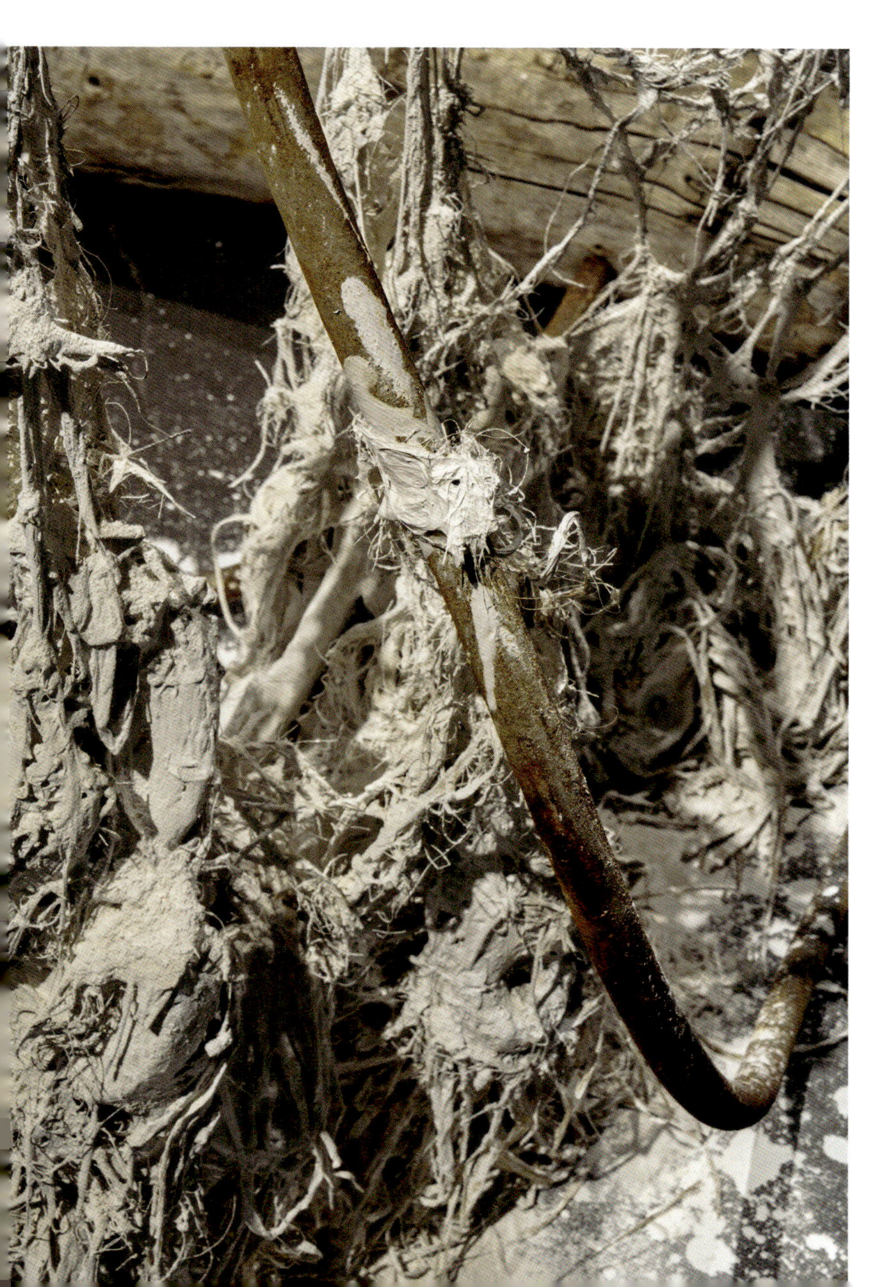

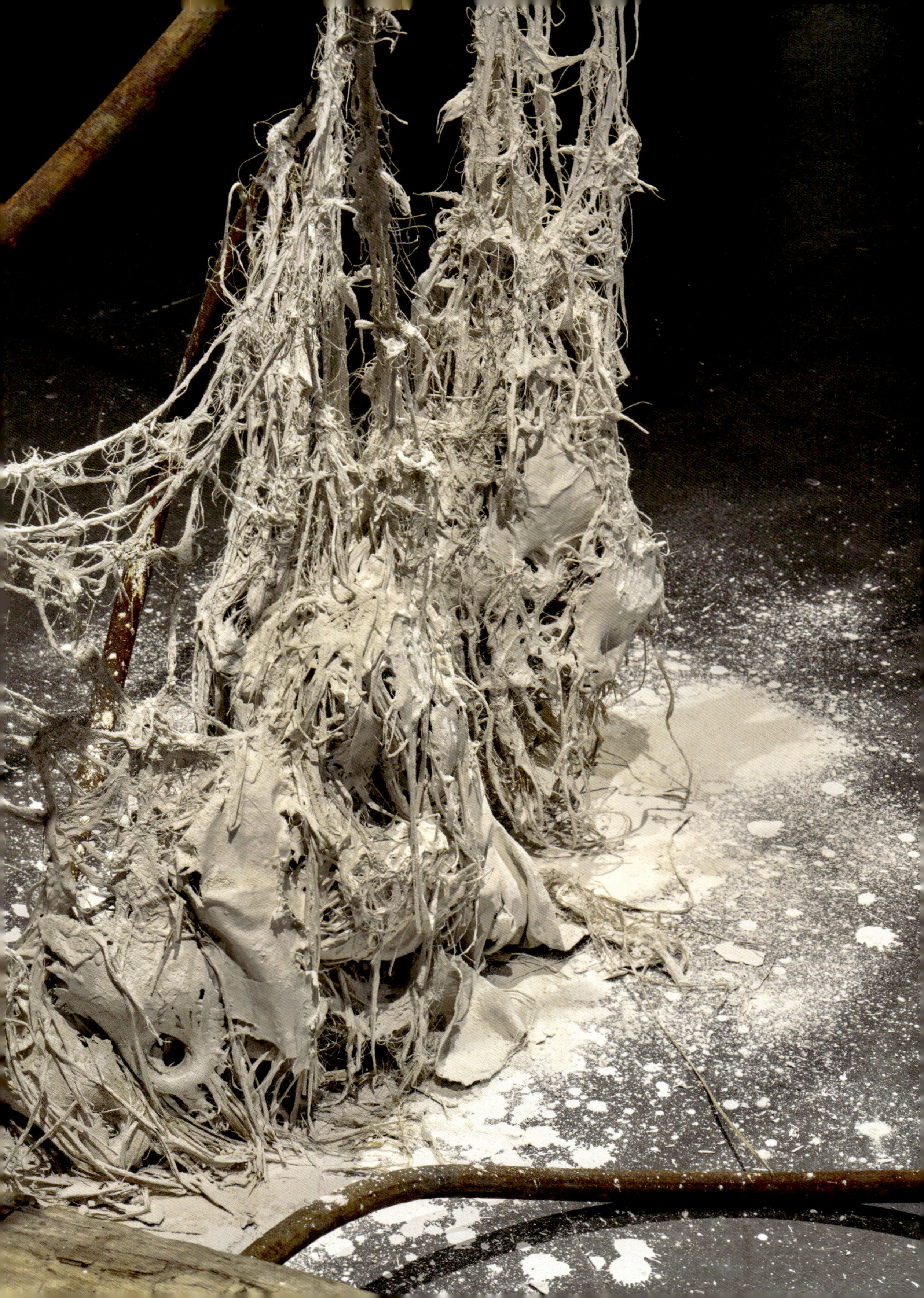

INTO THE DEEP

DOMINIQUE WHITE AND
BINA VON STAUFFENBERG

NELLE PROFONDITÀ

Dominique White has been creating her new work, *Deadweight*, as a direct result of her Max Mara Art Prize residency in 2023–24. It is to date the most radical expression of her ongoing concerns and ideas and pushes her practice to a new level. The following conversation reveals the thinking behind White's ephemeral and poetic sculptures and explores new elements particular to *Deadweight*.

BINA VON STAUFFENBERG   I believe the most natural starting point for a conversation about your work is the sea. Water is central to your work. I understand that your preoccupation with water started as a very personal journey of mourning but developed into a kind of universal mourning, looking at how global power dynamics today are built on colonial legacies in general and the slave routes and transatlantic trade in particular. Could you talk about this transition from a personal to a general concern?

DOMINIQUE WHITE   To me, the sea has always been an alternate world, an underworld, a spiritual realm and a site for the dead. I used to speak often of the Kalunga line, the horizon that splits the living from the dead, and I still find solace in the idea that perhaps my soul or spirit will return to spend eternity under the limitless waves, instead of being bound to a landmass.

The sea is also a site of impossibility, a flattening of time and a rejection of order. These are the ideas that my ongoing thesis, 'Shipwreck(ed)' (2018–), is rooted in, a practice rooted in ongoing mourning that has evolved into a revolt or rebellion against land. The sea is a site of more fantastical and unfathomable Afrofutures that reject the notions of the colonisation of tangible matter (see Elon Musk and his quest to colonise Mars versus the Black Planet[1]) and that blur the definition of the Human or humanoid.

BVS   Can you give a brief explanation of what Afrofuturism means for your work?

DW   I like to say it's like an impossible future. When I use the word impossible, I don't mean that it's impossible to achieve; it's just impossible to *imagine* under the current constraints of society. It's something that goes completely against the current depiction of the future or ideals of capitalism, the nation-state and so on. It's an undoing of all of that.

1   Referring to the political rap album *Fear of a Black Planet* by Public Enemy (1990).

Dominique White ha realizzato la sua nuova opera *Deadweight*
in seguito alla residenza del Max Mara Art Prize for Women nel
2023-24. Ad oggi l'opera costituisce l'espressione più rappresentativa
delle sue idee e interessi, portando la pratica di White a un nuovo
livello. La conversazione che segue rivela le riflessioni sottese alle
sculture effimere e poetiche di White ed esplora nuovi elementi
che sono specifici di *Deadweight*.

BINA VON STAUFFENBERG Ritengo che il punto di partenza più
naturale per iniziare una conversazione sul tuo lavoro sia il mare.
L'acqua è centrale nel tuo lavoro. So che il tuo forte interesse
per l'acqua è iniziato come un percorso di elaborazione del lutto
personale, poi evolutosi in una sorta di lutto universale, avendo
osservato come le odierne dinamiche del potere globale si basino
sulle eredità coloniali in generale e sulle rotte degli schiavi e sul
commercio transatlantico in particolare. Potresti parlare di questa
transizione da un interesse personale a uno universale?

DOMINIQUE WHITE Per me il mare è sempre stato un mondo alternativo,
un mondo sommerso, un regno spirituale e un luogo per i morti. Avevo
l'abitudine di parlare spesso della *Kalunga line* - la linea dell'orizzonte
che divide i vivi dai morti - e trovo ancora conforto nell'idea che forse
la mia anima o il mio spirito torneranno a trascorrere l'eternità tra le
infinite onde, invece di rimanere confinati alla terraferma.

Il mare è anche un luogo di impossibilità, di appiattimento del tempo
e di rifiuto dell'ordine. Queste sono le idee su cui si basa la mia ricerca
tuttora in corso, "Shipwreck(ed)" [Naufrag(i)o] (2018-in corso), una pratica
radicata in un continuo cordoglio che si è trasformato in una rivolta, o
ribellione, contro la terra. Il mare è un luogo di fantasiosi e insondabili
afrofuturi che rifiutano le idee di colonizzazione dello spazio (si veda
Elon Musk e il suo tentativo di colonizzare Marte contro il *Black Planet*[1]
[Pianeta nero]), e che sfumano la definizione di Umano o umanoide.

BVS Puoi spiegare brevemente cosa significa l'afrofuturismo
per il tuo lavoro?

DW Mi piace dire che è un futuro impossibile. Quando uso la parola
impossibile, non intendo dire che sia impossibile da realizzare. È
solo impossibile da *immaginare* considerando i vincoli odierni della
società. È qualcosa che va completamente contro la rappresentazione

1   Si fa riferimento all'album di rap politico *Fear of
a Black Planet* del gruppo Public Enemy (1990).

BVS Is it a utopian science fiction?

DW Somewhat. But I don't know whether utopian is the right word to use, because I think there are many different versions of futures. This is why I tend to reference music quite a lot, like Busta Rhymes – everything about the Black future that he is dreaming of or depicting is on fire.[2] He and his crew are the only ones who have survived, and they are now reigning supreme in the next era – whatever that is, as we don't really know. (I'm sure there's already a term that defines the post-Anthropocene, but let's dream of something beyond that.) It's not exactly like a utopia in its most traditional definition.

Another example of this utopia, in an untraditional sense, is Drexciya and the nation of Drexciya, which is birthed from the trauma of the Middle Passage.[3] A nation of people born in water and who, therefore, can breathe underwater.

I'd also challenge the use of the term 'science fiction' when referring to Afrofuturism as it tends to imply a detachment from reality and is rooted solely in the speculative. We carve out smaller, possible Black futures on the daily just through our persistence to continue living and rebelling against the status quo. The more 'impossible' futures that are often spoken of require a different approach to just surviving.

BVS Your works have been described as 'monuments to Black lives lost and utopian bridges to an imaginary underwater world where Blackness is freed and untamed'. Here is another quote: that your practice expresses a 'desire for the destruction of the metaphorical slave ship's hull in which modern Blackness was conceived and remains'.[4] Would you say these are accurate observations?

DW One can escape the hull and build something new, but one will always be bound to the order of land. It is inevitable that recapture and/or mutation of the hull will occur – it's something that we've witnessed generation after generation across the world. We are currently bearing witness to another mutation of imperialism, of mass disabling, mutilations and genocide – it often does resemble an unstoppable 'killdozer'.[5] I can only see it getting worse, due to the alarming rate at which technology is being developed for destruction versus the amelioration of life.

In order to think of a Black future, you would have to pulverise the hull, destroy this ship in its entirety beyond recognition. It's why I became disillusioned with the idea of Afrofuturism in Outer Space,

5   The Killdozer refers to an armoured, tank-like bulldozer adapted by Marvin Heemeyer and driven through Granby, Colorado, on 4 June 2004, wrecking or damaging a number of buildings.

4   Olamiju Fajemisin, 'Flights of Fantasy: Dominique White', *Mousse*, no. 79 (March 2022) (moussemagazine.it/magazine/dominique-white-olamiju-fajemisin-2022).

2   Busta Rhymes (b. 1972) is an American rapper, songwriter, record producer and actor.
3   Drexciya was an American electronic music duo from Detroit, Michigan, consisting of James Stinson (1969–2002) and Gerald Donald (b. 1980).

attuale del futuro o dei principi del capitalismo, dello Stato nazionale e così via. È un annullamento di tutto questo.

BVS È come una fantascienza utopica?

DW In un certo senso, ma non so se utopico sia la parola giusta da usare, perché penso che ci siano molte versioni diverse di futuro. Per questo motivo tendo spesso a citare la musica, ad esempio Busta Rhymes[2]: tutto ciò che lui raffigura o sogna per il futuro nero è entusiasmante. Lui e la sua squadra sono gli unici sopravvissuti e ora regnano sovrani nella prossima era – qualunque essa sia, dato che non lo sappiamo davvero (sono sicura che esista già un termine che definisce il post-Antropocene, ma sogniamo pure qualcosa che vada oltre). Non è esattamente un'utopia nella sua definizione più tradizionale.

Un altro esempio di questa utopia, in un senso anticonvenzionale, è quello di Drexciya[3] e la nazione di Drexciya, nata dal trauma del *Middle Passage* [passaggio di mezzo]. Una nazione di persone nate nell'acqua e che, quindi, possono respirare sott'acqua.

Contesterei anche l'uso del termine "fantascienza" quando ci si riferisce all'afrofuturismo, poiché questo tende a presupporre un distacco dalla realtà ed è radicato esclusivamente in una riflessione speculativa. Ogni giorno ci ritagliamo piccoli futuri neri possibili soltanto attraverso la nostra perseveranza, continuando a vivere e a ribellarci contro lo status quo. I futuri più "impossibili", di cui si parla spesso, richiedono un approccio diverso dalla semplice sopravvivenza.

BVS Le tue opere sono state descritte come "monumenti alle vite nere spezzate e ponti utopici verso un immaginario mondo sottomarino in cui la 'Blackness' è liberata e indomita". Un'altra citazione afferma che la tua pratica artistica esprime il "desiderio di distruggere il metaforico scafo della nave negriera in cui è stata concepita e in cui permane la moderna 'Blackness'".[4] Ritieni che queste siano osservazioni corrette?

DW Si può evadere dallo scafo e costruire qualcosa di nuovo, ma si sarà sempre legati all'assetto della terraferma. È inevitabile che si verifichi una riconquista e/o un mutamento dello scafo – è qualcosa a cui abbiamo assistito generazione dopo generazione in tutto il mondo. Attualmente siamo testimoni di un altro cambiamento dell'imperialismo, un cambiamento di massa invalidante, di mutilazioni e di genocidi – è qualcosa che spesso assomiglia a un inarrestabile "killdozer".[5] Vedo solo che la situazione peggiora, a causa del ritmo

2 Busta Rhymes (nato nel 1972) è un rapper, cantautore, produttore discografico e attore statunitense.

3 I Drexciya erano un duo di musica elettronica americano di Detroit, Michigan, formato da James Stinson (1969–2002) e Gerald Donald (nato nel 1980).

4 Olamiju Fajemisin, 'Flights of Fantasy: Dominique White', *Mousse* 79, marzo 2022. Se non diversamente specificato, la traduzione in italiano dei testi originali è curata dalla traduttrice.

5 "Killdozer" fa riferimento a un bulldozer blindato simile a un carro armato, trasformato da Marvin Heemeyer e guidato attraverso la città di Granby, in Colorado, il 4 giugno 2004, distruggendo o danneggiando diversi edifici.

as we are actively witnessing a new era of colonisation and slavery emerge. We can't outrun them forever.

BVS So you don't think it has to stay contained? You want the revolution, you want the rebellion, you want to explode the hull?

DW Yes. I think that's why I also struggle with being labelled as an Afropessimist or a Black nihilist, as I don't think the current situation is the only end point. Sure, some of my thinking is certainly rooted in this, especially when my heart feels especially squeezed, but the 'Shipwreck(ed)' looks beyond that moment. I don't think a future is possible without destroying the hull, and I'm certain its destruction is possible. It's just a matter of *when* it will happen, not if.

BVS Hydrarchy is another term that is being used in relation to your work, describing the idea of the sea as the basis of power systems that are still in place today.

DW Hydrarchy is a word from the 1600s, coined by the English poet Richard Braithwaite (1588–1673). It describes the ability to gain power and wealth through the instrument of water. I like to explore it in the inverse. The idea is those deemed as cargo or as having limited value within the ship – pirates, runaway slaves, slaves and others – can overthrow the hierarchy on board and therefore destroy order on land. Hydrarchy from below was a very true threat in the late 1600s and 1700s, and I often wonder what the world would have been like if they had succeeded.

BVS Let me pick up the term 'Shipwreck' and move to the visual form and materiality of your work. Your sculptures and installations appear ephemeral, poetic, fragile. However, the process of getting there is the opposite. It is marked by a distinct brutality: you wield, you smash, you burn, and now you will even submerge in water. How intentional and important is this contrast for you?

DW Very. I'm very interested in this idea of disrupting the power dynamic between object and viewer. I think when it comes to object making, especially, we're taught to keep the viewer and the audience in mind – in the sense that the viewer will always have the power. For me, the tension between the actual heaviness of the work, the materials and the process of creating them, and their seemingly fragile appearance is where the disruption of power happens. It's almost like a self-defence

allarmante con cui la tecnologia viene sviluppata per distruggere la vita anziché per migliorarla.

Per immaginare un futuro nero, bisognerebbe polverizzare lo scafo, distruggere questa nave nella sua interezza e renderla irriconoscibile. È per questo che sono diventata disillusa rispetto all'idea dell'afrofuturismo nello spazio cosmico, dal momento che stiamo assistendo in prima persona all'emergere di una nuova era di colonizzazione e schiavitù. Non possiamo sfuggirgli per sempre.

BVS Quindi non pensi che debba rimanere circoscritto? Vuoi la rivoluzione, vuoi la ribellione, vuoi far esplodere lo scafo?

DW Sì. Credo che questo sia il motivo per cui mi trovo in difficoltà quando vengo etichettata come un'afropessimista o una nichilista nera, perché non credo che la situazione attuale sia l'unico punto di arrivo. Certo, alcune delle mie posizioni sono radicate in questa direzione, soprattutto quando mi si stringe particolarmente il cuore, ma il "Shipwreck(ed)" ["Naufrag(i)o"] guarda oltre questo momento. Non credo che un futuro sia possibile senza distruggere lo scafo e sono certa che la sua distruzione sia possibile. È solo questione di *quando questo accadrà*, non se accadrà.

BVS Idrarchia è un altro termine utilizzato in relazione al tuo lavoro, descrive l'idea del mare come il fondamento dei sistemi di potere ancora oggi in vigore.

DW Idrarchia è una parola del Seicento, coniata dal poeta inglese Richard Braithwaite (1588–1673). Descrive la capacità di conquistare potere e ricchezza attraverso lo sfruttamento dell'acqua. Mi piace, tuttavia, affrontare la questione all'inverso. L'idea è che coloro che sono considerati merci o di scarso valore all'interno della nave - si pensi a pirati, fuggitivi, schiavi e altri simili - possano rovesciare la gerarchia a bordo e quindi distruggere l'assetto della terraferma. L'idrarchia dal basso era una minaccia molto reale tra la fine del Seicento e il Settecento, e spesso mi chiedo come sarebbe stato il mondo se avesse avuto successo.

BVS Riprendo il termine *"naufragio"* per soffermarmi sulla forma visiva e sulla materialità del tuo lavoro. Le tue sculture e installazioni appaiono effimere, poetiche, fragili. Tuttavia il loro processo di realizzazione è l'opposto. È caratterizzato da una spiccata brutalità: vengono manipolate, colpite, bruciate, e ora saranno anche immerse nell'acqua. Quanto è intenzionale e importante per te questo contrasto?

mechanism in the work – if you get too close, it might either destroy itself or harm the viewer. There's a menace within the fragility.

> BVS Let's look a little closer at the intense physical process of creating your work. It's partly dictated by the materials you choose, but I also feel there's an element of anger that fuels the production.

DW Yes, there's definitely anger when I produce, but it's also a result of using very unruly and rigid materials. I have, for example, worked with mahogany, one of the hardest woods to try to steam and bend. (The force alone has ripped a lot of my fingernails out.) Another example is working with iron. Physically, it's obviously a solid material, but at the same time it's soft and volatile to some extent. It's impossible to control everything that will happen when I'm working with iron. You always have to expect the unexpected. I always say that I'm a mediator of the materials, because there's only so much you can really control. As a result, there can be anything from fractures or tears to works completely collapsing when there's too much pressure. I really like pushing things to their extremes. And in doing so, it pushes my body to its extreme.

> BVS Do you think that this tension between fragility and brutality has something to do with the vulnerability versus the resilience of Blackness?

DW Absolutely. I see my work as interventions in what is historically a very white, conservative space. This tension you mention is a refusal to play by the rules, to be stable.

> BVS This brings us to the project that you are creating as a result of your Max Mara Art Prize for Women residency, *Deadweight*. Can we start by talking about the title?

DW The title came from a book I was reading at the time of writing the proposal. It was the first time I had seen a term that really embodied the idea of rebellion on the ship. I was looking for a term or an idea that really encapsulated this idea of destroying the ship from within.

Similar to hydrarchy, the idea is to turn the definition of deadweight on its head: deadweight (tonnage) is a unit used to measure how much weight a ship can carry. It is the sum of the weights of cargo, fuel, fresh water, ballast water, provisions, passengers and crew. Instead of using it to ensure the ship stays afloat and moves seamlessly, I want to use it to

DW   Moltissimo. Mi interessa profondamente quest'idea di spezzare
la dinamica di potere tra oggetto e spettatore. Penso che, soprattutto
nella realizzazione di oggetti, ci venga insegnato di non dimenticare
l'osservatore e il pubblico, nel senso che lo spettatore avrà sempre il
potere. Per me, la tensione tra l'effettiva pesantezza dell'opera, i materiali,
il processo di creazione e il loro aspetto apparentemente fragile è il punto
in cui il potere viene spezzato. È quasi un meccanismo di autodifesa
dell'opera: se ci si avvicina troppo, potrebbe distruggersi o ferire lo
spettatore. C'è una minaccia all'interno della fragilità.

BVS   Esaminiamo un po' più da vicino l'intenso processo fisico
di creazione delle tue opere. In parte è dettato dai materiali che
hai scelto, ma credo anche che ci sia un elemento di rabbia che
alimenta la produzione.

DW   Sì, c'è sicuramente rabbia quando produco, ma è anche dovuto
all'uso di materiali rigidi e ostici. Per esempio, ho lavorato con il
mogano, un legno tra i più difficili da piegare a vapore – la sua sola forza
mi ha spezzato spesso le unghie. Un altro esempio è il lavoro con il
ferro: è ovviamente un materiale duro, ma allo stesso tempo è morbido
e in qualche modo imprevedibile. È impossibile controllare tutto ciò che
accade quando lavoro con il ferro. Bisogna sempre aspettarsi l'inaspettato.
Dico sempre che sono una mediatrice dei materiali, perché non c'è molto
che si possa davvero controllare. Il risultato è che può verificarsi qualsiasi
cosa, da crepe o strappi fino al collasso completo delle opere quando
c'è troppa pressione. Mi piace molto spingere la materia al suo estremo,
portando di conseguenza anche il mio corpo al suo estremo.

BVS   Pensi che questa tensione tra fragilità e brutalità abbia a che
fare con la vulnerabilità e la resilienza della "Blackness"?

DW   Assolutamente. Vedo il mio lavoro come un intervento in uno spazio
storicamente molto bianco e conservatore. La tensione a cui ti riferisci
è un rifiuto a giocare secondo le regole, a essere stabili.

BVS   Questo ci porta al progetto che hai creato in seguito alla
tua residenza per il Max Mara Art Prize for Women, *Deadweight*.
Possiamo iniziare parlando del titolo?

DW   Il titolo deriva da un libro che stavo leggendo al momento della
redazione della proposta. Era la prima volta che incontravo un termine

figure out its tipping point, which is the possibility to sink it, destroy it and free its cargo in the process.

    BVS What about material and form?

DW The forms of these works are something I've never created before, which both excites me and scares me – for good reasons. It's good to be scared.

    BVS The sculptures look more angular, more sharp, not as organic and flowing as anything I've seen in your work before. How did this evolve?

DW I think it came from the references I was working with when I was in Todi. In the studio there, I had a huge reference board, which is where the works all derived from. The angular forms you're referencing come from a lot of unique anchors I came across. There were stacks and stacks of these anchors, just left rotting, in all these fishing villages near Genoa. I was obsessed with them! I set out to replicate them myself, distorting them from their original use.

    BVS So they're going to make up one work?

DW Yes. They'll be stacked and clumped together. The other three works are based on what's called the ship's cradle. It's something that came from my time in Genoa, where I learned how a ship is built in both a historical and contemporary sense. It starts with a cradle that consists of a spine and ribs, resembling a sea mammal's carcass. During my time at the University of Genoa, I understood that a lot of shipbuilding terminology refers to birth, life and death. It's super fascinating to see how many nautical terms derive from parts of the human body, almost like this object is coming to life.

    BVS Is that process characteristic of the way you work? You build up a library of references consisting of theoretical texts, poetry, music, found objects, followed by sketches and decisions on materials?

DW Yes, it's quite a long and intense process. I spent most of last year working six or seven days a week, whether that was collecting reference images, researching, drawing or building works. The references were

che incarnasse davvero l'idea di ribellione sulla nave. Cercavo un termine o un'idea che comprendesse realmente questo concetto di distruzione della nave dall'interno. Come per l'idrarchia, l'idea è quella di capovolgere la definizione di "deadweight" [portata lorda]: il tonnellaggio di portata lorda è un'unità di misura utilizzata per calcolare il peso che una nave può trasportare. È la somma dei pesi di merci, carburante, acqua dolce, acqua di zavorra, provviste, passeggeri e equipaggio. Invece di usarla per garantire che la nave rimanga a galla e navighi senza problemi, voglio usarla per capire il suo punto di ribaltamento, ovvero la possibilità di affondarla, distruggerla e liberarne il carico.

BVS E per quanto riguarda il materiale e la forma?

DW Le forme di queste opere sono qualcosa che non ho mai creato prima: questo, per buone ragioni, mi entusiasma e mi spaventa allo stesso tempo. È bello essere spaventati.

BVS Le sculture sembrano più spigolose e taglienti, non così organiche e fluide come quelle che ho visto in precedenza nel tuo lavoro. Come si è evoluto questo aspetto?

DW Penso che sia stato determinato dalle fonti con cui lavoravo quando ero a Todi. Nello studio avevo un'enorme bacheca piena di riferimenti, da cui derivano tutte le opere. Le forme angolari a cui ti riferisci provengono da tantissime ancore - uniche nel loro genere - in cui mi sono imbattuta. In questi villaggi di pescatori vicino a Genova c'era un'infinità di ancore ammucchiate e lasciate a deteriorarsi: sono diventate una mia ossessione! Mi sono impegnata a riprodurle, alterandole rispetto al loro uso originale.

BVS Quindi diventeranno un'opera unica?

DW Sì. Saranno impilate e raggruppate insieme. Le altre tre opere si basano su quello che viene chiamato scafo di una nave. È un'idea nata durante il mio soggiorno a Genova, dove ho imparato come si costruisce una nave sia nella sua accezione storica che contemporanea. Si parte da uno scafo composto da una spina (o chiglia) e da costole (o ordinate) che ricordano la carcassa di un mammifero marino. Nel tempo che ho trascorso all'Università di Genova ho capito che gran parte della terminologia navale si rifà alla nascita, alla vita e alla

objects I saw in day-to-day life, in books, in the archives or strewn
across the docks of whichever city I was in. They all found their
way into numerous sketchbooks and then manifested as drawings
of possible sculptures. Often, I must concede that, in terms of
physics, some structures would just collapse on themselves.

> BVS Am I right in saying that, so far, you haven't made any
> work that you can't physically move yourself?

DW Yes, that's why the heavier sculptures come apart in sections.
I always have to think about the logistics and practicalities before
embarking on the actual production. Sure, the work can be 6 metres
tall, but the doorframe is only 2.3 metres tall – rather boring problems!
Sometimes I produce and install at the same time, like in my recent
show at Kunsthalle Münster.[6] Everything was cast and built on the
spot, very intensely. I dream big but ensure I lay out the groundwork
to make it possible.

> BVS For *Deadweight,* you've actually submerged the iron elements
> of the sculpture in the Mediterranean Sea for the first time in your
> practice. In what ways is that a natural next step in your practice and
> where do you hope to go with that?

DW Throughout my practice, submerging the works has always been
a romantic, unrealistic idea for the futurity of the works. It's the idea
that if you put the majority of my practice back in the water, everything
except for the iron and the wood would dissolve and disappear almost
immediately. All that would be left would be these kinds of harpoons
floating in the sea. Obviously I can't do that. But by submerging the
iron, I'm pushing the limitations of the work into this kind of unknown
realm. Iron is used extensively in ports or next to the sea, and you often
see that, after fifty or a hundred years of continuous exposure, the iron
swells and develops this red, puffy surface. You cannot control what
seawater does to iron once it's submerged.

> BVS Let's talk about how the experience of working in two different
> Italian bronze foundries influenced the development of *Deadweight*.

DW It was a privilege to meet and work alongside Fonderia di Campane
Marinelli in Agnone and Fonderia Artistica Battaglia in Milan, as they
both embody such different eras of technique within Italian bronze work.

6 'Dominique White: When Disaster Strikes', Kunsthalle Münster, 8 December 2023–10 March 2024.

morte. È molto affascinante notare come molti termini nautici derivino da parti del corpo umano, quasi come se questo oggetto stesse prendendo vita.

BVS Questo processo è caratteristico del tuo modo di lavorare? Raccogli un catalogo di riferimento composto da testi teorici, poesia, musica, oggetti trovati, a cui seguono disegni preparatori e la scelta dei materiali?

DW Sì, è un processo piuttosto lungo e intenso. Ho trascorso la maggior parte dell'anno scorso lavorando sei o sette giorni alla settimana, indipendentemente che si trattasse di raccogliere immagini di riferimento, fare ricerche, disegnare che di costruire le opere. I riferimenti erano oggetti che trovavo nella vita quotidiana, nei libri, negli archivi o disseminati sui moli portuali di qualsiasi città in cui fossi. Hanno tutti trovato spazio in svariati taccuini, diventando poi disegni di possibili sculture. Spesso, devo ammetterlo, in termini di fisica alcune strutture sarebbero semplicemente crollate su loro stesse.

BVS È vero che finora non hai mai realizzato opere che tu stessa non potessi spostare fisicamente?

DW Sì, è per questo che le sculture più pesanti vengono scomposte in pezzi. Devo sempre pensare agli aspetti logistici e pratici prima di intraprendere la produzione vera e propria. Certo, l'opera può essere alta 6 metri, ma lo stipite della porta è alto solo 2,3 metri: problemi piuttosto noiosi! A volte produco e allestisco allo stesso tempo, come nella mia recente mostra alla Kunsthalle di Münster[6]. Tutto è stato fuso e assemblato insieme sul posto, con grande concentrazione. Sogno in grande, ma prima verifico di aver posto le basi per renderlo possibile.

BVS Per *Deadweight* hai immerso gli elementi in ferro della scultura nel Mar Mediterraneo per la prima volta nella tua pratica artistica. In che modo questo rappresenta una naturale evoluzione della tua pratica? E dove speri di arrivare con questo passaggio?

DW Nel corso della mia pratica, l'immersione delle opere è sempre stata un'idea romantica e irrealistica rispetto alla condizione futuribile delle opere. È l'idea per cui se si rimettesse in acqua la maggior parte del mio lavoro, tutto, tranne il ferro e il legno, si dissolverebbe e scomparirebbe

6 'Dominique White: When Disaster Strikes', Kunsthalle Münster, 8 dicembre 2023–10 marzo 2024.

The Marinelli family, who have been working as bell producers in Agnone for nearly a thousand years, still use very similar techniques to their ancestors, so it truly was a rare opportunity to engage with such a historical practice. I could quite literally see the layers of history throughout their workshop, through handling tools that were perhaps older than the country of Italy itself. In working in their workshop, it almost felt like I was meddling with time. Somehow I was in 1423 and 2023 at the same time. It's rare to see intuition take centre stage in such a dangerous process; it's more than second nature, it was almost as if the materials themselves were whispering and guiding their decisions.

I also spent a week with the team at Fonderia Artistica Battaglia, who represent the experimental, contemporary energy in the bronze scene in Europe. Here they have perfected the more conventional lost-wax technique of their predecessors, and they're pushing the very limits of this technique through extreme experimentation. I clicked almost immediately with the team at Battaglia for this reason, as I'm a little infamous for applying the same mentality to object making in the studio. However, the more familiar I became with bronze, the more I found it to be a material that, in essence, is too laden with qualities that do not correlate just yet with my practice. For example, as ridiculous as it sounds, it's an incredibly permanent material.

BVS And in addition, bronze of course has many historical and art historical connotations.

DW Yes. We use bronze to represent people of power or people whom the state seeks to immortalise. Of course, bronze isn't the only material that has a long, stable life, but I find it jarring that we can uncover bronze statues at the bottom of the sea from 3,000 years ago, in near perfect condition. Bronze is so wrapped up in the politics of immortality that I almost think it would be too predictable. It's a very long-lasting and stable material that does not have a place in my discourse right now. I'm interested in the more volatile quality that I can find in iron or copper. I feel like this slipperiness is what gives my practice its own autonomy.

BVS   We've talked about many influences in your practice: theories of Afropessimism and Afrofuturism, the music and ideas of Busta Rhymes and Drexciya, robust materials with the inherent quality to transform and change. To finish our conversation, I'd like to draw attention to the three writers whose work you have chosen to feature alongside your work. Can you talk about how the writings of Olamiju

quasi immediatamente. Rimarrebbero solo queste specie di arpioni che galleggiano nel mare. Ovviamente non posso farlo, ma immergendo nell'acqua il ferro, spingo i limiti dell'opera in una sorta di regno sconosciuto. Il ferro è molto utilizzato all'interno dei porti o vicino al mare e spesso si può notare che, dopo 50 o 100 anni di esposizione continua, il ferro si dilata e sviluppa una patina rossa e rigonfia. Non si può controllare l'effetto dell'acqua marina sul ferro una volta che questo è stato immerso.

BVS Parliamo ora di come la tua esperienza di lavoro all'interno di due diverse fonderie di bronzo italiane abbia influenzato lo sviluppo di *Deadweight*.

DW È stato un vero privilegio conoscere e lavorare con la Pontificia Fonderia di Campane Marinelli ad Agnone e con la Fonderia Artistica Battaglia a Milano, dal momento che ciascuna incarna una diversa epoca di lavorazione del bronzo in Italia. La famiglia Marinelli, che ad Agnone produce campane da oltre mille anni, utilizza ancora tecniche molto simili a quelle dei suoi antenati: è stata davvero una rara opportunità di confronto con una pratica tanto antica. Ho potuto quasi vedere le stratificazioni della storia all'interno del loro laboratorio, maneggiando strumenti forse più antichi dell'Italia stessa. Lavorando nella loro officina mi è sembrato quasi di giocare con il tempo: in qualche modo mi trovavo nel 1423 e allo stesso tempo nel 2023. È raro trovare l'intuizione al centro di un processo così pericoloso: si tratta di più di un'istintività, era quasi come se i materiali stessi sussurrassero e guidassero le loro decisioni.

Ho trascorso una settimana anche con la Fonderia Artistica Battaglia, che nel panorama della lavorazione del bronzo in Europa emana energia sperimentale e contemporanea. Qui hanno perfezionato la più tradizionale tecnica a cera persa ereditata dai loro predecessori, spingendo oltre i limiti questa tecnica attraverso una sperimentazione estrema. Per questo motivo sono entrata quasi subito in sintonia con il team di Battaglia, dato che sono altrettanto nota per applicare la stessa logica alla realizzazione di oggetti in studio. Tuttavia, più prendevo confidenza con il bronzo, più mi accorgevo di quanto fosse, in sostanza, un materiale troppo ricco di qualità che semplicemente non sono legate alla mia pratica. Per esempio, per quanto possa sembrare ridicolo, è un materiale incredibilmente durevole.

Fajemisin and Alexis Pauline Gumbs and the poems of June Jordan
have influenced or inspired *Deadweight*?

DW   Each of these individuals has taught me new ways to rebel, resist
and imagine an outside. There's so much power held in their words, and
'inspire' would be too weak a word to describe the energy each of them
evokes within me. I would perhaps describe the sentiment as someone
embracing you and picking you up when you are too weak to walk. There's
a sense of community in their words, a rallying cry to act. It's through
this community that I am the artist I am today. To survive in this world,
you must surround yourself with the troublemakers, the rebels and the
nonconformists. I wouldn't want it any other way.

Dominique White and Bina von Stauffenberg were in conversation
between Marseille and London, 29 February 2024.

BVS Inoltre, il bronzo ha molte connotazioni storiche
e storico-artistiche.

DW Sì, usiamo il bronzo per rappresentare persone di potere o persone
che uno stato desidera rendere immortali. Certo, il bronzo non è l'unico
materiale che ha una vita lunga e durevole, ma trovo sconcertante che si
possano ritrovare in fondo al mare statue di bronzo di 3.000 anni fa, in
condizioni quasi perfette. Il bronzo è talmente coinvolto nella questione
dell'immortalità che mi sembra quasi troppo prevedibile. È un materiale
talmente duraturo e stabile che non trova posto nel mio discorso attuale.
Mi interessa una qualità più volatile che posso trovare nel ferro o nel
rame: mi sembra che questa scivolosità sia ciò che conferisce alla mia
pratica una propria autonomia.

BVS Abbiamo parlato di molte influenze nella tua pratica: le teorie
dell'afropessimismo e dell'afrofuturismo, la musica e le idee di
Busta Rhymes e Drexciya, i materiali resistenti con la qualità
intrinseca di trasformarsi e cambiare. Per concludere la nostra
conversazione, vorrei richiamare l'attenzione sui tre scrittori il cui
lavoro hai scelto di affiancare al tuo. Puoi raccontare di come gli
scritti di Olamiju Fajemisin e di Alexis Pauline Gumbs e le poesie
di June Jordan abbiano influenzato o ispirato *Deadweight*?

DW Ciascuno di questi individui mi ha insegnato nuovi modi di
ribellarmi, di resistere e di immaginare un mondo esterno. C'è così
tanta forza nelle loro parole, e "ispirare" sarebbe un termine troppo
debole per descrivere l'energia che ciascuno di loro suscita in me.
Forse descriverei questo sentimento come se qualcuno ti abbracciasse
e ti prendesse in braccio quando sei troppo debole per camminare.
C'è un senso di comunità nelle loro parole, un entusiasmante appello
all'azione. È grazie a questa comunità che sono diventata l'artista
che sono oggi. Per sopravvivere in questo mondo, è necessario
circondarsi di piantagrane, ribelli e anticonformisti. Non vorrei
che fosse in altro modo.

Dominique White e Bina von Stauffenberg hanno conversato
tra Marsiglia e Londra il 29 febbraio 2024.

BIOGRAPHIES / BIOGRAFIE

SHOWS AND FAIRS / MOSTRE E FIERE

2024   *Deadweight* [solo]. Whitechapel Gallery, London, and Collezione Maramotti, Reggio Emilia

2024-5   *Sous L'Azur.* Art Explora, Marseille (travelling)

2024   *Destruction of Order* [solo]. VEDA, Florence

2024   *Dominique White and Alberta Whittle: Sargasso Sea.* ICA Philadelphia

2023-4   *When Disaster Strikes…* [solo]. Kunsthalle Münster, Münster

2023-4   *Phantom Sculpture.* Warwick Arts Centre, Coventry

2023   *Fugitive of the State(less)* [solo]. ART CITY, Bologna

2023   *May you break free and outlive your enemy* [solo]. La Casa Encendida, Madrid, curated by Pakui Hardware

2022-3   *Afterimage.* MAXXI L'Aquila, curated by Alessandro Rabottini and Bartolomeo Pietromarchi

2022   *Statements* [solo]. Art Basel 2022, Basel

2022   *Love.* Bold Tendencies, London

2022   *cinders of the Wreck/les cendres du naufrage* [solo]. Triangle France, Marseille

2021-2   *Hand to your ear Part 1 (presence/surplus).* Emalin, London, curated by Gabriella Nugent

2021-2   *Hydra Decapita* [solo]. VEDA, Florence

2021   Solo presentation with VEDA. Artissima, Turin

2021   *Becoming Fugitive State* [solo]. Bloc Projects, Sheffield

2021-6   *Techno Worlds.* Art Quarter Budapest, Budapest (travelling)

2021   *Blackness in Democracy's Graveyard* [solo]. UKS, Olso

2020-21   *Possédé·e·s.* MO.CO, Montpellier, curated by Vincent Honoré

2020-21   *Mere Skyn.* CAPC, Bordeaux, curated by Cory John Scozzari

2019   Presentation with Aviva Silverman. Paris Internationale

2019   *Boundary + Gesture.* Wysing Arts Centre, Cambridge, curated by Taylor Le Melle

2019   *Abandon(ed) Vessel.* Kevin Space, Vienna

2019   Solo presentation. Art-O-Rama, Marseille, winner of the Roger Pailhas Prize

2019   *Fugitive of the State(less).* VEDA, Florence

2018   *Flood-tide.* Love Unlimited, Glasgow

2018   *The Share of Opulence; Doubled; Fractional.* Sophie Tappeiner, Vienna, curated by Cédric Fauq

2018   *°c.* Clearview.ltd, London

2018   *Signs | Beacons.* Caustic Coastal, Manchester

2017   *Allen Road Sculpture Park.* Artlicks, London, curated by Graft Lancaster

2017   *A Study in Devotion.* MARKET Peckham, London

2017   *The Other'd Artist/s.* Transmission, Glasgow, curated by Travis Alabanza

2017   *12o Collective.* Online

2017   *In Search of Our Mothers' Gardens.* Copeland Park & Bussey Building, London

OLAMIJU FAJEMISIN is an art critic. Her writing has been published by periodicals including *Artforum, Frieze, Flash Art* and *Mousse Magazine.* She has also produced exhibition texts and catalogue essays for a number of international galleries and institutions, such as Gladstone Gallery and Haus der Kunst. She has been an editor at Zurich-based publication PROVENCE since 2018. She studied at the Courtauld Institute of Art, London, and the Sandberg Instituut, Amsterdam, where she was awarded the Holland Scholarship.

ALEXIS PAULINE GUMBS is a queer Black feminist, love evangelist and an aspirational cousin to all life. She is the author of four books, including *Undrowned: Black Feminist Lessons from Marine Mammals,* which won the 2022 Whiting Award in Non-Fiction. A recipient of the Windham-Campbell Prize in Poetry, the National Endowment of the Arts Creative Writing Fellowship and a National Humanities Center Fellowship. Gumbs lives and loves in Durham, North Carolina. Audre Lorde is one of the great ancestral loves of her life.

BINA VON STAUFFENBERG is a freelance curator, writer and art advisor. She works with artists and private collectors in Europe and Latin America. Her particular interest is in artists who deal with political tropes or have been marginalised for their gender or race. She is the Jury Chair for the ninth edition of the Max Mara Art Prize for Women 2022–24, and has worked with each of the artist recipients since the inception of the Prize in 2005. She holds a MA in Contemporary Art and is a former Associate Director of Christie's.

OLAMIJU FAJEMISIN è una critica d'arte. I suoi scritti sono stati pubblicati da periodici come *Artforum, Frieze, Flash Art* e *Mousse Magazine.* Ha inoltre scritto testi per mostre e cataloghi di numerose gallerie e istituzioni internazionali, come Gladstone Gallery e Haus der Kunst. Dal 2018 è redattrice presso la casa editrice PROVENCE di Zurigo. Ha studiato al Courtauld Institute of Art di Londra e al Sandberg Instituut di Amsterdam, dove ha ottenuto la Holland Scholarship.

ALEXIS PAULINE GUMBS è una femminista nera queer, predicatrice dell'amore ed un'aspirante amica di tutte le forme di vita. È autrice di quattro libri, tra cui *Undrowned: Black Feminist Lessons from Marine Mammals,* vincitore del Whiting Award 2022 per la saggistica. Vincitrice del Windham–Campbell Prize per la poesia, della borsa di studio di scrittura creativa National Endowment of the Arts e della borsa di studio National Humanities Center. Gumbs vive e ama Durham, in North Carolina. Audre Lorde è uno dei grandi atavici amori della sua vita.

BINA VON STAUFFENBERG è curatrice, scrittrice e art advisor freelance. Lavora con artisti e collezionisti privati in Europa e in America Latina. Il suo interesse è rivolto in particolare agli artisti che si occupano di questioni politiche o che sono stati emarginati per il loro genere o razza. È presidente della giuria della nona edizione del Max Mara Art Prize for Women 2022–24 e ha collaborato con tutte le artiste che hanno ricevuto il premio sin dall'inizio nel 2005. Ha conseguito un master in arte contemporanea ed è stata direttore associato di Christie's.

ACKNOWLEDGEMENTS / RINGRAZIAMENTI

DOMINIQUE WHITE
WOULD LIKE TO THANK /
DESIDERA RINGRAZIARE
Shantelle Palmer
Alexis Pauline Gumbs
The Estate of June Jordan
Olamiju Fajemisin
Deborah Joyce Holman
Ima-Abasi Okon
Eva Duerden
Taylor LeMelle
Gianluca Gentili
Claudia Cucca
Katrina Schwarz
Bina von Stauffenberg
Jennifer Lauren Martin
Emii Alrai
Claudia Tacchella
Giovanna Fiume
Alessandro Rametta, Andrea
    Capriotti and the team at
    La Fucina di Efesto
Michele Ciribifera and
    Sofia Bianchini
The participants of
    An Environment for Black
    Feminism: History, Theory,
    Aesthetics' workshop at
    University of Copenhagen
    (June 2024)
A Practice for Everyday Life
Sophie Kullmann

COLLEZIONE MARAMOTTI,
WHITECHAPEL GALLERY
AND / E MAX MARA WOULD
LIKE TO THANK / DESIDERANO
RINGRAZIARE
For the residency /
Per la residenza
Agnone
    Pontificia Fonderia di
    Campane Marinelli
Palermo
    Giovanna Fiume
    Irene Matranga
    Palazzo Butera
Genova
    Massimo Corradi
    Claudia Tacchella
Milano
    Fonderia Artistica Battaglia
Todi
    Michele Ciribifera
    Metalserbatoi s.n.c.
For the production /
Per la produzione
La Fucina di Efesto
    Marina Genova

MAX MARA ART PRIZE JURY /
GIURIA 2022–24
Bina von Stauffenberg,
    Jury Chair / Presidente
    della giuria
Rózsa Farkas,
    Gallerist / Gallerista
Claudette Johnson,
    Artist / Artista
Derica Shields,
    Writer / Scrittrice
Maria Sukkar,
    Collector / Collezionista

The Whitechapel Gallery would like to thank its supporters, whose generosity enables the Gallery to realise its pioneering programmes / Whitechapel Gallery desidera ringraziare i suoi sostenitori, la cui genorisità permette alla Galleria di realizzare i suoi programmi innovativi.

MAJOR DONORS AND SUPPORTERS
Arts Council England Catalyst Endowment Fund
Sir Frank Bowling
Bloomberg Philanthropies
D. Daskalopoulos Collection
Ford Foundation
Foyle Foundation
Freelands Foundation
Collezione Maramotti
Max Mara
Paul Mellon Centre for Studies in British Art
The Rose Foundation
Terra Foundation for American Art
Michael and Nina Zilkha

EXHIBITIONS PROGRAMME A/POLITICAL
Aldgate Connect BID
Erin Bell
Cockayne – Grants for the Arts
Anton Kern Gallery
Igor and Anastasia Bukhman
Richard Chang
Collezione Maramotti
De Ying Foundation
Martin and Rebecca Eisenberg
Fluxus Art Projects
Selma Feriani Gallery
Goodman Gallery
Green Family Art Foundation
Oliver Haarmann

Hauser & Wirth
Hiscox
Institut français of Paris
Max Mara
Kate MacGarry
Mennour, Paris
Paul Mellon Centre for Studies in British Art
Rennie Collection
Richard Saltoun Gallery
Craig Robins
Tony and Elham Salamé
Maria and Malek Sukkar
Gary Steele and Steven Rice
Vielmetter Los Angeles
Michael Zilkha
The Whitechapel Gallery Commissioning Council
The Whitechapel Gallery Patrons
and those who wish to remain anonymous

EDUCATION AND PUBLIC PROGRAMMES
The 29th May 1961 Charitable Trust
Aldgate Connect BID
Capital Group
Kurt Forrest Foundation
Phillips
Tower Hamlets Arts and Music Education Service (THAMES)
The London Borough of Tower Hamlets
Stanley Picker Trust
The Whitechapel Gallery Education Council

WHITECHAPEL GALLERY CORPORATE PATRONS AND MEMBERS
Alma
Bloomberg Philanthropies
Frasers Property UK
Gazelli Art House

Lisson Gallery
Phillips

WHITECHAPEL GALLERY CORPORATE SUPPORTERS
Aldgate Connect BID
Bloomberg Philanthropies
Champagne Pommery
Crozier Fine Arts
Fedrigoni
Hiscox (Artworks Insurance Partner)
Max Mara
Collezione Maramotti
Omni Colour (Signage Partner)
Phillips

WHITECHAPEL GALLERY COMMISSIONING COUNCIL
Dorota Audemars
Erin Bell
Émilie De Pauw
Irene Panagopoulos
Nicole Saikalis Bay

WHITECHAPEL GALLERY EDUCATION COUNCIL
Julie and Debashis Dey
Alex Sainsbury

WHITECHAPEL GALLERY GLOBAL CIRCLE
Yan Du
Elie Khouri Art Foundation
and those who wish to remain anonymous

WHITECHAPEL GALLERY DIRECTOR'S CIRCLE
Erin Bell and Michael Cohen
Pilar Corrias
Julie and Debashis Dey
Rami Kim
Bimpe Nkontchou
Anthea Peers
Katie and Felix Robyns

Thatcher and Jill Thompson
and those who wish
    to remain anonymous

WHITECHAPEL GALLERY
CURATOR'S CIRCLE
Annette Anthony
Adrian and Jennifer O'Carroll
Oba Nsugbe
Audrey Wallrock
and those who wish
    to remain anonymous

WHITECHAPEL GALLERY
PATRONS
Malgosia Alterman
Cedric Bardawil
Sadie Coles HQ
Francesca Consigli
Sarah Elson
Joanna and Alan Gemes
Mark Harris
Pippy Houldsworth
Marie Krauss
Frank Krikhaar
Kate MacGarry
Mary E McNicholas
Heike Moras
Maureen Paley
Dominic Palfreyman
Darryl de Prez and
    Victoria Thomas
Maria-Cruz Rashidian
Marina Roncarolo
Marina Ruiz-Colomer
Alex Sainsbury and Elinor Jansz
Cherrill and Ian Scheer
Veronica Schwabach
Elisabeth von Schwarzkopf
Amar Singh
Karen and Mark Smith
Bina and Philippe von Stauffenberg
Christoph and Marion Trestler
Sharon Zhu and Michael Tian
and those who wish
    to remain anonymous

We remain grateful for the
ongoing support of Whitechapel
Gallery Members / Siamo grati
per il continuo supporto dei
membri di Whitechapel Gallery.

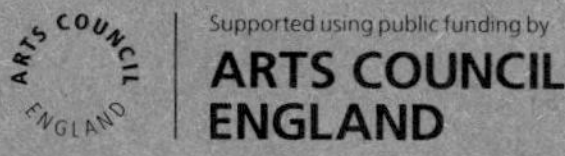

The Whitechapel Gallery is
proud to be a / è fiera di essere
National Portfolio Organisation
of Arts Council England.

Published on the occasion of
the exhibition / Pubblicato in
occasione della mostra
Max Mara Art Prize for Women:

Dominique White · *Deadweight*

Whitechapel Gallery, London:
　2 July / luglio–15 September /
　settembre 2024
Collezione Maramotti,
　Reggio Emilia:
　27 October / ottobre 2024–
　16 February / febbraio 2025

EXHIBITION / MOSTRA

WHITECHAPEL GALLERY
Director: Gilane Tawadros
Curator, Special Projects:
　Katrina Schwarz
Gallery Technical Manager:
　Luke Edwards
Installation Coordinator:
　Neftalí Carreira

COLLEZIONE MARAMOTTI
Director: Sara Piccinini
Max Mara Art Prize for Women
　Project Manager:
　Giulia Cirlini

WHITECHAPEL GALLERY STAFF
Syara Ahmed, Shohid Ahmed,
Sadika Begum, Fatima Begum,
George Bird, Olivia Blyth, Sue
Bowley, Daniel John Bracken,
Neftalí Carreira, Christy Chan,
Elizabeth Clowes, Claudia
Contu, Joel Cosson, Camilla
Cuminatti, Harry Curtoys, Pedro
da Costa, Anh Tuan Dao, Helen
Davison, Asa Desouza-Jones,
Alan Diamond, Aggie Dolan,
Colette Downing, Luke Edwards,
Molly Evans, Gabriella
Fabbriani, Misha Faulty, Lao
Farrant, Shirin Fathi, Will
Ferreira Dyke, Cameron Foote,
Freya Gascoyne, Alejandra
Gissler, Olivia Gomes, Luke
Gregory-Jones, Majharul Islam,
Yulia Ivanova, Carolina Jozami,
Jacqueline Kent, Hana Munirah
Khan, Andrey Lazarev, Kirsty
Lowry Smith, Ewa Luc, Aili
Markelius, Richard Martin,
Colette McNulty-Andrews,
Katerina Mesterovic, Luis
Mondejar, Gemma Murray,
Rummana Naqvi-Ladak, Jade
Nicklin, Amelia Oakley, Pianka
Pärna, Elsie Plimmer, Natasha
Plowright, Katherine Proudlove,
Alice-Anne Psaltis, Agostino
Quaranta, Raffia Rahman,
Mabrur Rahman, Martin Reyes,
Ella Ross-Leahy, Rishika Sahgal,
Jane Scarth, Katrina Schwarz,
Francesca Scott-Sills, Sadie
St Hilaire, Vicky Steer, Allan
Struthers, Tamanna Sultana,
Sean Synnuck, Gilane Tawadros,
Alice Thompson, Katie Town,
Lucie Treinen, Muhammad
Uddin, Drupesh Vekaria,
Thomas Watson, Sam Williams,
Yuk Wun Jade Wong, Hiu Ching
Florence Wong, Hannah Woods,
Andrea Ziemer-Masefield